Abbey Lubbers, Banshees & Boggarts

Also by Katharine Briggs

The Personnel of Fairyland
The Anatomy of Puck
Folktales of England
The Fairies in Tradition and Literature
British Folktales
An Encyclopedia of Fairies
The Vanishing People

Abbey Lubbers, Banshees & Boggarts

An Illustrated Encyclopedia of Fairies

Katharine Briggs

Illustrated by Yvonne Gilbert

Pantheon Books
New York

Copyright © 1979 by Katharine Briggs

Illustrations Copyright © 1979 by Yvonne Gilbert

All rights reserved under International and Pan-American Copyright Conventions. Published in the United States by Pantheon Books, a division of Random House, Inc., New York. Originally published in Great Britain by Kestrel Books.

Library of Congress Cataloging in Publication Data

Briggs, Katharine Mary.
    Abbey lubbers, banshees, and boggarts.

    An abridged and simplified version of the author's Encyclopedia of fairies, which was originally published under title: A dictionary of fairies.
    Bibliography: p.
    SUMMARY: A "Who's Who" of fairyland, with entries by fairy name and additional legends, songs, and anecdotes within each entry.
    1. Fairies—Dictionaries.   [1. Fairies—Dictionaries]   I. Gilbert, Yvonne.   II.   Briggs, Katharine Mary. A dictionary of fairies.

GR549.B742   1979   398.2′1′03   79-1897
ISBN 0-394-50806-8

The author and publishers wish to thank Mr. Frederick Grice for permission to include the story about a "duergar" (pp. 62-64), which first appeared in his *Folk Tales of the North Country* (Nelson, 1944).

Manufactured in the United States of America

First American Edition

I dedicate this book to you
Dear Katharine Law, who always knew
How best to cheer and bear me through
An author's toils;
And to say true,
She cheered and helped the artist too.

INTRODUCTION

THIS book is a shortened form of *A Dictionary of Fairies* (published in the U.S.A. as *An Encyclopedia of Fairies*). There are fewer articles but some of them are longer than those in the Dictionary, because there are more anecdotes and tales about the fairies in this book than in the earlier one. If you want to know something about the people who researched into fairy beliefs, or about the opinions held about them by the folklorists, or by the country people who really believed in fairies, you will have to look in the *Dictionary of Fairies*.

The Fairies of these Islands are of all kinds. There are good and bad. (In Scotland these are called the "Seelie Court" and the "Unseelie Court".) There are the big and the little, the beautiful and the ugly, the trooping fairies and the solitary fairies. Some of them only look beautiful by glamour – that is the magical power by which fairies can make humans see what they want them to see by a kind of optical illusion – but they are thin and wizened to anyone whose eyes have been opened by rubbing them with fairy ointment. Even the appearance of fairy food and fairy houses is sometimes changed by this power. According to the old beliefs there were quite a lot of things one had to be careful about if one met even a good fairy. For instance, the passage of time was different in fairyland, and people who thought they had been dancing in a fairy ring for about half an hour would find when they got out that a year had passed, or it might even be two hundred years. If they ate food in fairyland they might never be able to get out at all, because they had become fairies themselves.

The kind fairies would often give mortals precious gifts; but if people told about the gifts they would disappear. Fairies, too, would sometimes work for mortals and help them in all sorts of ways; but if they were watched or spied upon they would go away and never come back. They were secret people.

In old days nearly all country people believed in fairies and thought it wise to be very cautious about offending even the good ones. Against the bad ones they used every kind of charm and protection they could devise: holy things, a cross and a Bible or even a page of Scripture, holy water and a piece of bread because the fairies were pagans, and iron, particularly a knife or a pair of scissors, for the fairies came from the Stone Age. And there were certain trees and plants that were a protection against them: rowan – that is, mountain ash – and ash trees and St John's wort and verbena and a four-leaved clover. Then the fairies could not cross southward-flowing water, and evil fairies were put to flight if one knelt down and prayed, as little Gerda did in "The Snow Queen". You will find many of these protections used in this book and you will see that one could make mistakes even with the good fairies; but, though they were frightened, people were fond of them and loved them and their merry ways, and many well-known dances and airs are said to have been learned from listening outside the fairy hills. The Londonderry Air is one which most people know.

The fairies on their side seem to have been dependent on humans. They needed human nurses and doctors to help in the birth of their children. Their own food too was not very nourishing, and they had to take the goodness out of human food, or actually steal it. They may have felt that they had a right to it, for they were fertility spirits who made the corn spring and fruits set and ripen, and they brought the flowers out of their buds and gave them their bright colours. There are some people who still believe this, but for the most part when we say, "That's not a real fairy story", we mean that it is not one that was ever really believed; it was just made up as a pretty fancy. There were a good many stories of that kind made up at the beginning of this century, and they had no solidity about them, but those that were made up by people who had heard the old stories told by countrymen, or who had studied the subject seriously, like George Macdonald or Professor Tolkien, are very different. The stories told by this kind of writer have a sense of reality about them, as if they gave your mind something to bite on.

Some of these fairy beliefs are very old, and we find good stories about them in the medieval chronicles, written down by the monks as early as the twelfth century. One of these is the story of King Herla, which you will find in this book, and which tells of the different rate of time in Fairyland. Another is about a bogey-beast called the Grant, and there is one about a little boy called Elidor who was playing truant from school and was taken by some kind little fairies into a fairyland under a waterfall, where he came and went freely until he stole a golden ball to show to his mother, and after that he never found his way back. Years after, when he had become a priest, he would tell all about the fairyland, and the little dogs and horses they had, and he was deeply grieved to think how ungrateful he had been to the kind little people.

At the end of this book there is a short list of books in which the originals of the tales I tell are to be found, including a few which tell us more about fairy beliefs.

I hope that you will enjoy the book, and perhaps become a folklorist, collect stories for yourself, and tell them to other people.

KATHARINE BRIGGS

Note: Every now and then in the articles you will find a fairy's name written all in capitals. This means that there is an article about that fairy, and you will find it in its proper alphabetical position if you want to read more about it.

Abbey Lubbers, Banshees & Boggarts

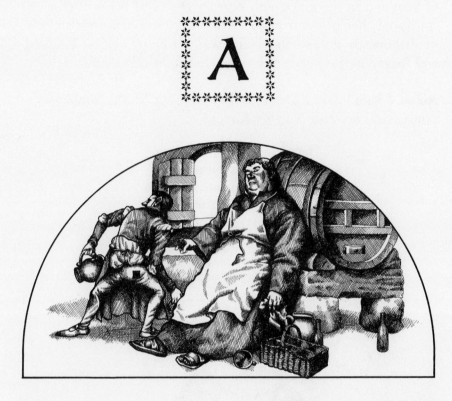

Abbey Lubber. In the later days of the monasteries, about the fifteenth century, when people generally believed that the monks had become worldly, lazy and corrupt, tales were told of abbey lubbers, minor devils who came where the monks were greedy and drunken and given to all sorts of jollity instead of praying and good works. Abbey lubbers feasted in the cellars and the kitchens and tempted the monks to all kinds of evil. A famous one was Friar Rush, about whom a chapbook was written. He was unmasked and driven out by the Prior, and after various adventures became a Will o' the Wisp. The monks were so shocked by what had happened that they reformed themselves and led virtuous lives ever afterwards, so Friar Rush had done good instead of evil, which must have been a disappointment to him. Tales were told too about the BUTTERY SPIRIT, who haunted inns where the innkeeper was dishonest, and ate up all his profits. In the Highlands of Scotland in the nineteenth century they still believed that evil spirits only had power over goods that were accepted unthankfully, or dishonestly got, so this belief was probably held in England, and indeed in the whole of Europe, in the Middle Ages.

Aiken Drum. Aiken Drum is best known as the subject of a nonsensical Scottish Nursery Rhyme:

> There cam' a man to oor toun,
> To oor toun, to oor toun,
> There cam' a man to oor toun,
> An' his name was Aiken Drum.

He wore all kinds of eatable clothes, a hat of cream cheese, a coat of roast beef and buttons of penny loaves, but there was a Border poet, William Nicholson, who gave the name of Aiken Drum to the BROWNIE who haunted Blednoch Farm, and *he* wore no clothes at all except a kilt of rushes. This Aiken Drum, like many other brownies, was driven away by a gift of clothing:

> For a new-made wife, fu' o' rippish freaks,
> Fond o' a' things feat for the first five weeks,
> Laid a mouldy pair o' her ain man's breeks
>   By the brose o' Aiken-drum.

> Let the learned decide when they convene,
> What spell was him and the breeks between;
> For frae that day forth he was nae mair seen,
>   And sair missed was Aiken-drum!

Ainsel. The story of Ainsel comes from Northumberland, but variations of it can be found in all kinds of places, beginning with the story of Ulysses and the Giant Polyphemus. A widow and her little boy lived in a cottage near Rothley. The boy always hated going to bed early, and one night he was so lively that his mother went to bed herself and left him still at play. She warned him that the fairies would carry him off if he sat up too late, but he only laughed, so she blew out her candle and left him to play by the light of the fire. After a little while a lovely little fairy girl came floating down the chimney. "What do they call you?" said the little boy, enraptured. "Ainsel," said the little fairy; "what do they call you?" "I'm my ainsel" – that's myself – "too," said the boy, and they began to play together merrily. Presently the fire burned low, and the boy stirred it up in such a hurry that a cinder flew out and burnt Ainsel's foot. At that she set up such shrieking that the boy was quite frightened and hid behind the wood-pile. Not an instant too soon, for with a great rumbling and rushing an old fierce fairy came down the chimney. "What ails ye, my hen?" she cried. "I'm brent, manny, I'm brent!" said the wee thing. "Who

brent ye?" said the mother fairy. "I'll sort him." "My ainsel."
"Your ainsel!" said the old fairy. "What call have ye to make such
a cry about it? Away up with ye!" and she kicked little Ainsel up
the chimney in front of her. The boy made one leap into the bed
beside his mother and covered his head with the bedclothes. It was
many a night before he sat up late again.

Apple-Tree Man. In Somerset the oldest apple-tree in the orchard
was called "the Apple-Tree Man", and it seems that the spirit of
the orchard was supposed to live in it. Years ago, when Ruth
Tongue was at school, she heard a story about the Apple-Tree
Man, and she recorded it for *The Folktales of England* in
1963. In this story the elder brother was the good character and
the younger brother was the bad one. It is about Christmas Eve,
when old people thought that beasts could talk and the ox and
the ass were sure to do so. This is the tale:

There was once a hard-working chap who was the eldest of a long
family, so he'd been out in the world working to keep himself since he
was a lad of twelve, and his father had almost forgotten about him. But
when all the rest had gone into the world the youngest had stayed in the
farm, petted and cossetted, and his father thought the world of him, and
when he died he left everything in the youngest son's hands as used to be
the custom in those parts. Well the youngest doled out bits and pieces of
things to all the family, but when it came to the eldest he only gave him
an old ox that was worn to a skeleton and his Dad's old donkey that was
dear knows how many years old, and he let him rent his Dad's old
tumble-down cottage that he had lived in with his grandfather, with a
few old, ancient apple trees standing round it, and he looked to have
that rent paid for on the dot too.

Well, the elder brother never grumbled, but he set to work to make
the best of it. He went out along the hedgerows, cutting all the good,
lush grasses, to feed the donkey with them, and the donkey begun to
fatten up wonderfully, and he rubbed the ox with herbs and said the
right words, and the old ox began to step out quite smartly and to look
a different creature; then he turned the two of them into the orchard to
graze, and to manure the ground, and those apple trees perked up until
it was a marvel to see them. But all this kept him too busy to earn any
wages towards the rent and he didn't know how he was to scrape it up.

Well one day the younger brother came into the orchard and said: "Tomorrow's Christmas Eve and come midnight all beasts do talk, they say. Now they all say there's a treasure hidden somewhere in this orchard, but none of us knows where, so I'm all set that I'll ask the old donkey, and he's bound to tell me if I ask him proper. So do you wake me in good time before twelve and I'll tell you what I'll do – I'll let you off sixpence of your rent."

And off he goes, quite pleased with himself.

Next morning was Christmas Eve, and the chap got up in good time and did a grand cleaning of the whole place. He stuck sprigs of holly in the shippen over the dunk's stall and the ox's. He made the house spick and span, and hauled in a good ash log for a Christmas faggot. He filled the mangers with a double feed of hay and tied up the dunk and the ox early to give them a good rest. Then he lighted the Yule log and warmed up the last little drop of cider he had and poured it over the root of the oldest apple tree. And the Apple-Tree Man called out to him from inside: "You take your spade and dig down under my old rotten root here, and see what you can see, for 'tis yours, and no one else's."

So the eldest son fetched his spade, and hidden under the root was a small chest filled with the richest gold. "You take it," said the Apple-Tree Man. "Take it and keep quiet about it." So the chap did just as he said. "And now," said the Apple-Tree Man, "Go and fetch your dear brother, for 'tis close on midnight."

So the youngest brother came running in a terrible hurry-push, and as he crept up to the stable there was a light coming from it, and the ox and the ass were talking. "Do you see yonder greedy fool?" said the dunk, "that's listening to we so unmannerly? He wants that we should tell him where the treasure is."

"And that's where he will never find it," said the ox, "for someone else have got it already."

And that was all that the youngest brother ever heard of the treasure.

Aughisky. The aughisky was the Irish water-horse, very like the EACH UISGE of the Scottish Highlands. They were supposed to come out of the sea and gallop along the shore or through the

fields. Anyone who could catch one and lead it away from the shore could use it as a splendid mount, but if it came within sight or sound of the sea it would gallop wildly into the depths and tear its rider to pieces.

Awd Goggie. Awd Goggie was a nursery demon, probably invented by careful mothers to keep children from stealing fruits. They used to warn their children to keep away from the fruit trees and berry bushes, "or Awd Goggie will get you". Awd Goggie looked like an enormous hairy caterpillar, big enough to eat children.

Banshee. The Irish banshee (pronounced like that, but written in Irish *bean si*) is the Celtic prophet of death, who wails before the death of any of her family. She is generally supposed to be the spirit of some beautiful maiden of the family who died before her time. If several of them wail together it foretells the death of some-one specially great or holy. The banshee is described as very pale, with long streaming hair and eyes fiery red from weeping. She wears a grey cloak over a green dress. People are rather proud of having a banshee in their family, for it shows that they belong to one of the old families of Ireland. In the Highlands of Scotland the banshees are called *bean-nighe*, that is, "the little washer by the ford", and they keen and wail by the riverside, washing the grave-clothes of those who are about to die. When a lot are seen together it means that there will be a terrible accident.

Barguest. The barguest is a North Country BOGIE or bogey-beast. They say that it is the same kind of creature as the padfoot and the HEDLEY KOW, and like them it can change its shape, but it is generally seen as a big black dog with fiery eyes, horns and a long tail. It is supposed to be very unlucky to see it, for it is a kind of BANSHEE. If anyone important was going to die it used to appear on a piece of waste land near Leeds, with all the dogs of the district howling after it. But it seems to have done no harm to the old man who saw it on his way home from the Grassington Well-Dressing one cold winter night. He made a very good story of the meeting.

You see, sir, I'd been clock dressing at Grassington, and I'd stayed rather late, and had maybe had a little sup of spirit, but I was far from being drunk, and I knew everything that happened. It was about eleven o'clock when I left, and it was late in the year, but a most beautiful night. The moon was very bright, and I never saw Kylstone Fell plainer in my life. Now you see, sir, I was passing down the mill lane, and I heard something come past me – brush, brush, brush, with chains rattling all the while, but I could see nothing; and I thought to myself, now this is a most mortal queer thing. And then I stood still and looked about me, but I saw nothing at all, nothing but the two stone walls at either side of the mill lane. Then I heard again this brush, brush, brush, with the chains, for you see, sir, when I stood still it stopped, and then, thought I, this must be a barguest that so much is said about; and I hurried towards the wooden bridge, for they say a barguest cannot cross running water; but, Lord, sir, when I got over the bridge, I heard this same again, so it must either have crossed the water or gone round by the spring head! And then I became a valiant man, for I was a bit frightened before; and, thinks I, I'll turn and have a peep at this thing; I went up the Great Bank towards Linton, and heard this brush, brush, brush, with the chains all the way, but I saw nothing. Then it ceased all of a sudden. So I turned back to go home; but I'd hardly reached the door when I heard again this brush, brush, and the chains going down towards the Holin House, and I followed it, and the moon there shone very bright, and I saw its tail! Then thought I, thou old thing, I can say I've seen thee now; so I'll get home.

When I got to the door there was a great thing like a sheep, but it was larger, lying across the threshold of the door, and it was all woolly; and I says "Get up!" and it wouldn't get up. Then I says, "Stir thyself!" and it wouldn't stir itself. And then I grew valiant, and I raised my stick to beat it; and then it looked at me, and such eyes, they did glower, and as big as saucers and like a striped woolly ball. First there were a red ring, then a blue one, then a white one, and then these rings grew less and less till they came to a dot! But I was not frightened of it, though it grinned at me fearfully, and I kept on saying, "Get up," and "Stir thyself," and the wife heard as how I was at the door, and she came to open it; and then this thing got up and walked off; for it was more frightened of the old wife than it was of me; and I told the wife, and she said it was the barguest; but I never saw it since, and that's a true story.

Bauchan *(buckaun)* **or Bogan.** A bauchan was a hobgoblinish spirit, sometimes helpful and sometimes mischievous. They seemed to get fond of their humans for there is one story of a bauchan who emigrated to America to be near his master.

Callum Mor MacIntosh had a little farm in Lochaber and there was a bauchan on the farm who was always fighting with Callum Mor, but was rather fond of him, and would help him at a pinch. For instance, one night when Callum Mor was returning home the bauchan attacked him and they had a fight. After they parted Callum found he had lost his favourite handkerchief, which had been blessed by the priest. He was sure the bauchan had taken it, so he turned back and found the bauchan rubbing it on a big rough stone. "Aha, Callum," said the bauchan, "it's as well you came back, I'd have been your death if I'd rubbed a hole in it. Now you'll have to fight if you want it." So they fought, and Callum got his handkerchief back. A little later when the snow came down, Callum had run out of firewood, and the snow was too deep for him to drag in a birch he had cut down. But as he was sitting at his dying fire there was a great thump at the door, and there was the birch, dragged all the way by the friendly bauchan. Some years later a great number of the Highlanders were taken

by force from their homes and shipped across the Atlantic. Callum Mor was one of the first. He had to stay some time in quarantine, and when at length he got to his plot of land, the first person who met him was the bauchan in the form of a goat. "Aha, Callum," he said, "I am here before you." And he was a great help to Callum in clearing the rough land.

Bendith y Mamau *(bendith er mamigh)*, **or the "Mother's Blessing".** This is a Glamorganshire name for the fairies. They are called this to please them, because they are supposed to be very eager to get hold of mortal children and to leave their own changelings or "crimbils" instead. The Bendith y Mamau were supposed to be stunted and ugly, so that they were very anxious to get hold of beautiful mortal children to improve their stock. There is a Welsh story. A young widow had a very beautiful baby whom she guarded with great care; the neighbours were sure that the Bendith y Mamau would try to steal it away. One day when the child was three years old she heard a great lowing among the cattle and ran out to see what was the matter. When she got back the cradle was empty, and a little, stunted boy was standing at the door who greeted her as "Mammy". She was sure he was a crimbil, for he never grew, and after a year she went to a cunning man, who told her that first she must test the child. To do this she got a raw egg and, taking it into the kitchen, cut the top off and stirred it up very carefully. When the crimbil asked her what she was doing she answered, "I am making a pasty for the reapers." "What!" he cried, "I heard from my father – and he heard it from his father and that one from his father – that an acorn was before the first oak; but I have neither heard nor seen anybody making the pasty for the reapers in an egg-shell!" The mother said nothing in reply, but that night she went and told the cunning man.

"So far so good," he said, "but we must now make sure that your own child is with the Bendith y Mamau." And he told her to go to the crossroads above Rhyd y Gloch four days after the full moon and watch there till midnight. The procession of the Bendith y Mamau would pass by then, and she must remain still and silent even if her child should be with them, or all would be lost. She

went and did just as he said, though her heart nearly burst when she saw her own dear son among the fairy children. Next morning she went to the cunning man and he told her to get a black cock without a white feather on it. She had a great search to find one, but she got it in the end. She wrang its neck and roasted it over the spit without plucking it. She did not look at the cradle until every feather had dropped off, then she turned round, and the cradle was empty, and outside the door she heard the voice of her own little son. He was thin and worn, and remembered nothing that had happened to him except that he had heard sweet music. He soon grew well and strong again, and they were never troubled by the fairies again. This is not the most usual way of rescuing a captive from Fairyland. Generally they have to be seized and held, and covered with a human garment.

Billy Blind. The name Billy Blind is only found in the traditional ballads. Billy means a companion or brother-in-arms. The Billy Blind was a HOBGOBLIN attached to a family, who gave good advice. The Billy Blind in the ballad of Young Bekie did more than that, for he provided a magic ship for Burd Isabel to cross the sea in time to prevent Young Bekie's marriage, and steered it himself. The Billy Blind in another ballad told a young husband how to break the spell that was laid on his wife so as to prevent the birth of her baby.

Black Annis. Black Annis, a cannibal hag with a blue face and iron claws, was once supposed to live in a cave in the Dane Hills in Leicestershire. It was said to have been dug out of the rock with her own nails, and was called "Black Annis' Bower Close". There was an oak tree near in which she hid, to jump out and catch children who passed near. Her name is sometimes connected with Anu, or Dana, one of the Mother Goddesses of Ancient Ireland. Gentle Annie, who called up storms in the Firth of Cromarty, may have been the same person. Ruth Tongue was told about Black Annis in 1941 by a little evacuee from Leicester. She published the story in *Forgotten Folk-Tales of the English Counties*.

Black Annis lived in the Danehills.

She was ever so tall and had a blue face and had long white teeth and she ate people. She only went out when it was dark.

My mum says, when she ground her teeth people could hear her in time to bolt their doors and keep well away from the window. That's why we don't have a lot of big windows in Leicestershire cottages, she can't only get an arm inside.

My mum says that's why we have the fire and chimney in a corner.

The fire used to be on the earth floor once, and people slept all round it until Black Annis grabbed the babies out of the window. There wasn't any glass in that time.

When Black Annis howled you could hear her five miles away and then even the poor folk in the huts fastened skins across the window and put witch-herbs above it to keep her away safe.

Black Dogs. Stories of black dogs are found all over the country. Sometimes they are helpful, but they are generally dangerous. As a rule the black dogs are large and shaggy, about the size of a calf, with fiery eyes. If anyone speaks to them or strikes them they have the power to blast, like the Mauthe Doog, the Black Dog of Peel Castle in the Isle of Man. In England, they are supposed to be the form taken by a human ghost. In Finstock in the Cotswolds there was a tradition of one that was laid with the help of prayers and a mother with a newly born child and a pair of clappers, used in scaring birds. There were two ponds in the village and one clapper was put into each pond. If ever those two clappers are put together it is said that the Finstock Black Dog will start his hauntings once more. At the beginning of this century stories were told of good black dogs who protected travellers from thieves, and sometimes they showed lost people the way. The Church Grim, who was a black dog buried in a new churchyard to guard it, looks after children, but scares away thieves and evil spirits. So the black dogs are not all bad.

Blue Burches. Blue Burches was a harmless hobgoblin who played BOGGART pranks in a shoemaker's house on the Blackdown Hills in Somerset. The cobbler's little boy was friendly with him, and had seen him once in his true shape, an old man in baggy blue "burches", or breeches. The cobbler and his family took all his pranks in good part. When heavy steps were heard descending the stairs and a wisp of blue smoke drifted across the room, the cobbler only said, "Never mind old Blue Burches; he never do no harm." And he went on proudly to boast of how Blue Burches ran across the room like a little black pig and jumped into the duck-pond without a splash, and how, when they were coming back late from market, he would set the house all a-glow to make them think it was on fire. He told his tale to the wrong audience, one of the churchwardens, who took old Blue Burches for the Devil himself and got a couple of parsons along to exorcize him. They came up and found an old white horse grazing by the duck-pond. "Who's that?" said the parson to the little boy. "That be old Blue Burches, sir," said the boy. "Can you put a bridle on him?" said the parson. The boy was proud to show how friendly old Blue Burches was, and he slipped the bridle over his head. At once both the parsons cried out together: "Depart from me, you wicked!" Old Blue Burches plunged into the pond and never came out again; at least, not in so friendly a form.

Blue-Cap. The blue-cap was a mine BROWNIE, who worked in the northern coal mines of England as a putter, that is, the man or boy used to push the filled tubs of coal. Unlike a brownie he expected to be paid for his work, but he would only take the ordinary wages of a putter; if he was given anything more he left it with scorn and if he was given less he left it all. But he did far more than an ordinary putter could do. As a rule he was not seen, only a blue light shone on a coal tub, and it moved along the rolly-way at a tremendous speed. A blue-cap was a friendly, lucky spirit to have in the mine, very different from some of the other mine GOBLINS.

Blue Men of the Minch. The Blue Men used particularly to haunt the straits between the Shiant Islands and Long Island. They swam out to wreck passing ships, but the Captain could overcome them if he could talk to them in rhyme and get the last word. It has been suggested that they were the spirits of Moors caught by Norwegian pirates and landed in Ireland in the ninth century. They were called "Blue Men" because they were tattooed blue. But some people thought they were real sea-spirits and that they caused the sudden storms that arose in the Shiant. They lived, like other sea-people,

in underwater caves, and were ruled by a chieftain. If they were captured they broke all the cords with which they were tied and escaped into the sea.

Boggart. A mischievous BROWNIE is called a boggart. Sometimes it is said that a boggart has a long, sharp nose and a brownie has no nose at all, only two little nostrils, but it seems that when a brownie is teased or misused he turns into a boggart and plays all sorts of mischievous tricks on the household, and it is very difficult to get rid of him. There is a story often told in a good many different places about a farmer who moved to get rid of the family boggart.

There was once a Yorkshire farmer called George Gilbertson whose house was much troubled by a boggart. He played his tricks on everyone about the place, and plagued the children worse than anyone. He would snatch away their bread and butter and upset their porringers, and shove them into corners and cupboards; and yet not a glimpse of him was ever seen. Perhaps the children did not mind him as much as the grown-up people, once they had got used to his ways. There was an "elf-bore" in one of the cupboards – that is a hole where a knot of wood had been – and one day the youngest boy stuck an old shoe-horn into it and it was pushed back so hard that it shot out of the hole and hit him sharply on the forehead. His mother was much distressed, but after this the children loved to play with the boggart by thrusting sticks into the hole and dodging them as they shot back. "Larking with the boggart", they called it. However the boggart's tricks got worse and worse, and poor Mrs Gilbertson became so anxious for the children that at last they decided to move, though they loved the old house. So on the day of their move their nearest neighbour, John Marshall, saw them following their last creaking carts out of the empty yard.

"And so you're flitting at last, George?" he said.

"Aye, Johnny lad, we're forced to it. That darned boggart torments us so that we can rest neither night nor day. It seems to have such a grudge against the poor bairns that it almost kills my poor dame at the thought of it. And so we're fair forced to flit."

And a great voice came booming out of the tall churn that stood in the last cart.

"Aye, Johnny lad, we're all flitting you see."

"It's that darned boggart!" said George. "If I'd a known you'd been there, you scoundrel, I'd never have stirred a foot. Turn back, Molly," he said to his wife. "We might as well be tormented in the old house as in another that's not so much to our liking."

So back they went, and the boggart played about their farm till he was tired of the sport.

Bogies. Bogies, bogles, bug-a-boos, and bogey-beasts are names given to a whole class of mischievous, frightening and even dangerous creatures whose delight it is to torment mankind. Sometimes they go about in hordes to frighten people in haunted castles or wild fen country, but most often they are solitary fairies, members of the UNSEELIE COURT. Dangerous though they are they are often easily tricked, just as the minor devils were in

33

medieval legends. The story of "The Bogie's Field" shows us one way in which this can be done.

Once there was a bogie that laid claim to a farmer's field, and after a long argument they decided that, though the farmer should do the work, they should divide the crop between them. So the first year in spring the farmer said: "Which will you have, tops or bottoms?"

"Bottoms," said the bogie.

So the farmer planted wheat; all the bogie got was stubble and roots. Next year he said he would have tops, and the farmer planted turnips; so he was no better off than before. He began to think he was getting the worst of it; so the next year he said: "You'll plant wheat, and we'll have a mowing match, and him who wins shall have it for keeps." "Agreed," said the farmer, and they divided the field up into two equal halves. But a little before the corn ripened, the farmer went to the smith and ordered some hundreds of thin iron rods, which he stuck all over the bogie's half of the field. The farmer got on like a house on fire, but the poor bogie kept muttering to himself, "Darnation hard docks, 'nation hard docks!" and his scythe grew so blunt that it would hardly cut butter. After about an hour he called to the farmer, "When do we wiffle-waffle, mate?" for in a reaping match all the reapers whet their scythes together.

"Waffle?" said the farmer. "Oh, about noon, maybe."

"Noon!" said the bogie. "Then I've lost," and off he went, and troubled the farmer no more.

Bogles. Bogles was the Scottish name for bogies, and very terrifying they could be, but some of the Border people thought that they were chiefly terrifying to evil-doers, and looked after those who were helpless. There is a story of a bogle who protected a poor widow from a neighbour who was stealing her candles. He used to creep into the shed where they were kept and the bogle booed and shouted at him, so he took a heavy stick and began to thrash about. But the bogle said, in a terrible voice, "I'm neither bone nor flesh nor blood; thou canst not harm me. *Give back the Candles!*" At that the man dropped the candles and fell on his knees. The bogle said, "I'll take something off you." And he

35

plucked a lash from the man's eyelid and that eye "twinkled ever afterwards".

Brag. The brag is one of the shape-shifting goblins, like the DUNNIE and the HEDLEY KOW. He belongs chiefly to Picktree in Northumberland, and generally goes about in the form of a horse, but he can change his shape as much as any of the goblins and bogies, except perhaps the Hedley Kow. Sometimes he turns himself into a calf with a handkerchief round his neck, or a naked man without a head, or a dick-ass or four men holding a white sheet, but he is most mischievous when he goes in his usual form as a horse, and tries to throw people off his back into ponds or streams.

Brown Man of the Muirs. The Brown Man of the Muirs was a Border spirit, who guarded wild animals but was the enemy of men because of the harm they did to his creatures. This is one of the stories told about him.

Two young men went out hunting on the moors near Elsdon in 1744. After shooting for some time they sat down to eat, and the youngest went to a burn near to quench his thirst. As he was drinking, the Brown Man of the Muirs came to the other side of the burn and shouted angrily to him. He was a stout fierce dwarf with red frizzled hair and great glowing eyes like a bull, and he scolded the boy furiously for killing the birds and beasts that were in his charge. "I eat only whortleberries and nuts and apples, and I'm as strong as a lion," he said. "Come and see." The lad was just going to jump the burn when his friend called to him not to cross the running water, and the dwarf disappeared. They both thought it likely that the Brown Man of the Muirs would have torn the lad in pieces if he had put a foot across the stream. They picked up their guns and bags and set off for home. On the way back the younger lad's spirits returned, and he began to boast of what he would have done if the dwarf had attacked him. Just then a bird got up and he raised his gun and brought it down. As it fell a stab of pain went through him. When he got home he took to his bed, and died after a short time. It was always believed that the Brown Man of the Muirs had taken revenge on him for his disobedience.

Brownie. Brownies are the best-known and the most widespread of the household HOBGOBLINS. They are little rough, hairy men who are to be found all over the Lowlands of Scotland, the North and East of England and down into the Midlands, though they are not so common there. Everywhere they come they help about the house during the night, and so long as their rules are kept they will work willingly for nothing except their small daily ration of food. But they can be touchy. Like most fairies they hate to be watched, and their work must not be criticized. The food given to them must be of good quality, but it must be left out for them to find for themselves; it is not etiquette to call a brownie's attention to a gift of any kind. They are almost always driven away by a gift of clothing. Different reasons are given for this. Sometimes it is said that the brownie is vain of his new clothes and runs away to show them in Fairyland, sometimes that he has been condemned to work for mortals until they think him worthy of a reward; sometimes he is offended by the poor quality of the clothes put out for him. For instance, in olden days there was a Lincolnshire brownie who used to grind meal and mustard, to clean up in the kitchen and do all sorts of odd jobs, in return for which, as well as his daily snack, the farmer used to put out a fine linen shirt for him every New Year. When the old farmer died, his son was too mean to waste good linen on a mere brownie and put out a coarse sacking shirt. The brownie put it on and capered about furiously, yelling so that all the house could hear him:

> "Harden, harden, harden hamp!
> I will neither grind nor stamp,
> Had you given me linen gear,
> I had served you many a year;
> Thrift may go, bad luck may stay,
> I shall travel far away."

And with that off he went, and never came back to the farm again. This is one story of many.

Different parts of the country give different names to the brownie. He is called "bwca" in Wales (see BWBACHOD), "bodach" in the Highlands of Scotland, FENODEREE in the Isle of Man, and PHOUKA in Ireland. The West Country PIXIES do household labours sometimes for mortals whom they like, just as the brownies do. If they are given clothes they go in the same way. There is a story of a little pixy who used to work for a poor young woman who had a drunken husband. As he worked the woman could hear him singing:

> "Little pixy, fair and slim,
> Not a rag to cover him."

It was no wonder she took pity on him and made him a nice suit of clothes. When he came in and saw it he put it on, capered about with joy, and sang:

> "Pixy fine and pixy gay!
> Pixy now will run away."

With that he ran off, and the poor young woman never saw him again.

You can imagine these fairy creatures of all shapes and sizes scattered about the country doing odd jobs for mortals until they are driven away by mean farmers or mischievous teasing boys or prying women, or by tactless attempts at charity.

Bucca, or Bucca-Boo. The Bucca is a Cornish spirit connected in some way with the sea. Fishermen used to leave a fish out for Bucca, and spill some of their ale on the ground so that Bucca should give them a good catch. So we can see that he was once a kind of fertility god. Later on, however, he degenerated into a bogie-beast to frighten naughty children. Mothers used to say, "You be quiet now and stop your crying, or Bucca-boo will come and carry you off." Some people say that there are two buccas, that is, Black Bucca and White Bucca; one is dangerous and the other good.

Buggane *(bug airn).* The buggane is the Manx bogey-beast and a very wicked character. He is a shape-shifter like the HEDLEY KOW, but much more dangerous and vicious. There are stories of one that used to live in Spooty Wooar, a big waterfall in the Patrick district. They say that many people saw him in times past, and not so far past either. He usually looked like a big black calf, which sometimes crossed the road and jumped down into the pool below the waterfall with a sound like clanking chains. But he could take a human form too, and then he was more dangerous. One day he came, looking like a tall man, to a house at the Glen May end of Glen Rushen where a servant lassie was sitting slicing up turnips. He picked her up, threw her over his shoulder and made off towards the waterfall. His house was in the hollow underneath the fall, and he meant to carry her off there and eat her. And that would have been the end of her, but fortunately she had kept tight hold of her turnip knife and just before the buggane jumped under the spout she cut her apron string by which he was holding her and jumped on to the land. You may be sure the houses up Glen May were carefully guarded with rowan-wood crosses after that escape.

Buttery Spirits. Buttery spirits are much the same as ABBEY LUBBERS except that they did not haunt abbeys but inns where the landlord was dishonest and big houses where the servants watered the wine and wasted and stole food. There is an old story of a landlord who was visited one day by his uncle, a very good old hermit.

"And how are things going with you, my boy?" said the hermit.

"Oh, they couldn't be worse, uncle," said the innkeeper. "I grow poorer and poorer every day, and yet I do all that I can to make money; I put water into every cask of wine, I mix sand with my sugar; I buy my meat cheap from beasts that have died; the guests' horses that I feed have chaff mixed with their oats, and yet for all that I can do I seem to lose money every day."

"Oh, that is bad," said the hermit. "Tell me, is there any window by which we can look into your larder without being seen?" "Yes, indeed there is," said the landlord. "If I open this little cupboard

I can see into the larder and keep watch to see that the servants are not stealing anything."

"Very well," said the hermit. "When you have opened the cupboard I will put my hand on your head and put your foot on my foot, and you will see what I see."

The landlord did so, and they peeped through the cupboard

together, and there they saw a buttery spirit, as fat as a pig, feasting on all the food in the larder, guzzling up the braxy meat and swilling away at the watered wine, and stuffing himself with the tasteless sweetmeats. The hermit shut up the window, and said to his nephew: "Son, spirits of that kind cannot eat honest food. Give your guests the best food you can find and the best service you can give them. Try no mean tricks to get rich. Act like an honest man and we will see how you have prospered when I come back next year."

In a year's time the hermit came back. His nephew looked brisk and thriving, the whole place was clean and polished, the servants were working with a will, the inn was full of customers. "Let us look through the cupboard this year, and see how things are now," said the hermit.

They looked through and saw a very different sight. The larder was crammed with good things and full bottles of wine were ranged on the shelves. And there was the poor buttery spirit, as thin as a cobweb, hardly able to drag itself along. It reached out for a fine pie near it, but it had no power to touch it; it put its mouth to a cask but nothing came; it tried a bottle of wine, but its hand went through it. The hermit shut the cupboard door. "I see you have been honest this year, my boy," he said. "Let nothing tempt you to dishonesty again, or you will be invaded by a crowd of evil spirits."

But the landlord had learnt his lesson. He lived honestly for the rest of his days.

Bwbachod. Bwbachod is the Welsh for the tribe of bwbachs and bwcas, the brownies of Wales. They are very like the brownies all over the country except that they have a particular dislike of tee-totallers and dissenting ministers. The bwcas seem to suffer particularly from mischievous boys and practical jokes. They revenge these by all kinds of tricks and in the end turn into down-right BOGGARTS and have to be banished to the Red Sea. There is a pathetic story told by one of the Welsh folklorists of a bwca who moved from farm to farm and was always teased and ill-treated until he became a regular boggart, and in the end was caught and banished to the Red Sea by a cunning man.

Cabyll-Ushtey. The cabyll-ushtey is the water-horse of the Isle of Man, as dangerous as the Highland water-horse, though not so many stories are told about it. There was a very wicked one who visited Kerroo Clough on the Dark River for a time. A farmer's wife found one of her calves missing, and next day the farmer saw a monstrous thing rise out of the river which seized one of the calves and tore it to pieces. They drove all the cattle far away from the river after that, but a far worse thing happened to them. Their daughter disappeared and was never seen again. After that the cabyll-ushtey left the river and never came back.

Cailleach Bheur *(cal'yach vare)*. The Cailleach Bheur of the Scottish Highlands, the blue-faced lean hag of winter, seems to have been a nature goddess once. There are many creatures rather like her, BLACK ANNIS of the Dane Hills, Gentle Annie of Cromarty Firth, Cally Berry in Ulster and the Gyre-Carline in the Lowlands of Scotland. In most legends about her, Cailleach Bheur seems to be the spirit of winter; she has a staff with which she touches the trees in late autumn, so that all the leaves fall. She roams the hills through the winter, herding the wild deer who are her cattle. Wild goats, swine and wolves were once in her charge, so, like the BROWN MAN OF THE MUIRS, she was the guardian of wild creatures. On the Eve of May Day she throws her staff under a holly tree and turns into a standing stone until she comes to life again on Halloween. (See illustration overleaf)

Capelthwaite. A Northumberland bogie who haunted the district of Milnthorpe used to be called "the Capelthwaite", and a barn near Beeston Castle is still called Capelthwaite Barn. He could take any shape he liked, but generally chose to appear like a black dog as large as a calf with fiery eyes. He was on good terms with the farm people and used to round up their sheep and cattle for them. The story was told of him, as of a good many willing, simple-minded hobgoblins, that he came in one evening, quite exhausted after his chase over the hills, and said he had had more trouble with the little brown lamb than with all the others put together. His lamb was a mountain hare.

The Capelthwaite, however, did not like strangers, and he was so spiteful and mischievous to them that at length the vicar laid him ceremoniously in the River Bela. Since then he has not been heard of, except by one man who came home late from the fair, capless, coatless and tattered, and told his wife that the Capel-thwaite had chased him everywhere and thrown him into the hedge. If his wife believed him his neighbours were not entirely convinced.

Cauld Lad of Hilton. The Cauld Lad of Hilton was one of those domestic spirits that are half Brownies, half ghosts. He was supposed to be the ghost of a stable-boy at Hilton Castle who had been killed long ago in a fit of passion by one of the lords of Hilton. Sometimes guests at the castle would be waked in the middle of the night by something very cold getting into bed beside them. It was the ghostly stable-boy. He was generally heard working in the kitchen at night, but he had a perverse habit of tossing about anything that was left tidy and tidying and cleaning anything that was left untidy or dirty. As he worked he sang sadly:

> "Wae's me, wae's me;
> The acorn's not yet
> Fallen from the tree,
> That's to grow the wood,
> That's to make the cradle
> That's to rock the bairn,
> That's to grow to a man,
> That's to lay me."

However, the time of his release was nearer than he knew, for the servants grew tired of the restless kitchen and laid out a cloak and hood by his bowl of bread and milk to pay him for his services. At twelve o'clock he put them on. Then he frisked about the kitchen, singing:

> "Here's a cloak and here's a hood,
> The Cauld Lad of Hilton will do nae mair good!"

And with the dawn he vanished for ever.

Changelings. Changelings were the things that were left to take the place of human babies or nursing mothers stolen by the fairies. From very early times we are told of the fairies' eagerness to get hold of human children. Tales of this are told in the medieval chronicles down to Elizabethan times and right on into this century. There are three different kinds of changelings. The first is a stock, a piece of roughly shaped wood, given by glamour an appearance of life, which gradually fades until it seems to die and is buried by the sorrowing relations. This is most generally used when a grown-up person is stolen – a nursing mother, needed to feed the fairy babies, or a beautiful young woman coveted by one of the fairy princelings.

The second changeling is a fairy baby which does not thrive. Human milk may give it a better chance, which may persuade the mother, while the other fairies would much prefer the beautiful mortal baby to bring fresh blood into Fairyland.

The third kind of changeling is one of the old, outworn fairies, tired of perpetual activity and only too glad to rest in his foster-mother's arms, fed, dandled and perpetually cossetted.

Sometimes the mother and the baby are both stolen, and then the first and second kinds of stock are used.

Sometimes when the changeling is a fairy baby its own mother wants it back again, and will help in the rescue. Lady Wilde gives a touching story of this in *The Ancient Legends of Ireland*. The fairies made a very daring raid against a new-born child. The father and mother were both asleep when the door burst open and a tall, dark man came into the house, followed by an old hag with a wizened, hairy child in her arms. The mother woke and called her husband, who jumped up and attacked the stranger. His candle was twice blown out, but he picked up the tongs and forced the old hag out of the house. They re-lit the candle, and then they saw that their own baby was gone and the hairy changeling was in its place. They burst out into lamentation, but the door opened and a young girl with a red handkerchief on her head came in. She asked them why they were crying, and when they showed her the changeling she laughed with joy and said: "This is my own child that was stolen from me tonight because my people wanted to take your beautiful baby, but I'd rather have ours; if you let me take it I will tell you how to get your child back."

They gave the changeling to her at once, and she told them to take three sheaves of corn to the fairy hill and to burn them one by one, threatening to burn every growing thing on the hill unless their baby was returned to them safe and well. This they did, and their child was given back to them at once. The fairies cannot bear to have the thorn-trees burnt on their hill.

When the changelings are very old, the first thing is to get them to betray their age. This is done by the "brewery of egg-shells". The mother makes up the fire and ranges a dozen or more empty egg-shells in front of it. She fills them up solemnly and puts a few grains of corn and one or two hops into each, and the thing in the cradle watches with more and more interest, until it bursts out with, "I have seen the first acorn before the oak, but I never saw brewing done in an eggshell before!" At that the mother heaps fuel on to the fire and throws the changeling into it, who flies laughing and shouting up the chimney.

This is one of the commonest methods, but there are other ways in which the changeling betrays himself. In Scotland it is often because he is always longing to play on the pipes.

The changeling belief has caused a great deal of suffering in its time. Often a child suddenly struck by an illness was suspected of being changed by the fairies and was ill-used so that the fairies would come and change the child back again. It was a sad life for any child that was suspected of being a changeling.

Clap-cans. Clap-cans is a Lancashire bogie and one of the least dangerous of that frightening class. He is called Clap-cans because of the noise he makes, like two cans being knocked together. This noise is the chief thing, indeed the only thing, about him. He cannot be felt or seen, he can only be heard.

Cluricaune *(kloor-a-cawn)* **or Cluracan.** The cluricaune is one of the solitary fairies of Ireland. Crofton Croker has several stories of him as a kind of BUTTERY SPIRIT, feasting himself in the cellars of drunkards or scaring dishonest servants who steal the wine. Sometimes he makes himself so objectionable that the house-owner decides to move, but the cluricaune pops into a cask to move with him, as the BOGGART did in Lancashire. The cluricaune described by Crofton Croker wore a red night-cap, a leather apron, pale blue long stockings and silver-buckled high-heeled shoes. His coat must have been red, for in Ireland the solitary fairies wore red coats while the trooping fairies wore green. (See illustration opposite)

Coblynau *(koblernigh)*. The coblynau are the Welsh mine goblins, not unlike the KNOCKERS of Cornwall. People say that they are about eighteen inches in height, dressed something like human miners and grotesquely ugly, though they are good-humoured and lucky to see and hear. By their knocking they lead miners to the best lodes of ore. If they are mocked they throw stones, but these do no harm. They always seem to be very busy, but actually they do nothing. This used to be said about the mine goblins in Germany too.

Coleman Gray. One day a Cornish farmer found a very small boy, cold, starved, miserable and apparently unable to speak English, hanging about close to his house. He was such a strange little thing that the farmer decided that he must be a pisky left on his doorstep to be cared for, so he took the little thing in and treated it as one of the family. Warmth, good food and kindness did wonders for it, and it soon became so merry and lively that they all loved it. It was tall enough to look over the half-door into the yard, and one day it was leaning on it, looking out rather sadly, when a voice was heard calling: "Coleman Gray! Coleman Gray!"

The pisky gave a great leap and clapped his hands. "My daddy's come! My daddy's come!" he cried, and he was gone in a moment, and they never saw him again.

Crodh Mara *(cro mara)*. Crodh mara, the Highland water-cattle, are much less dangerous than the Highland water-horse, EACH UISGE. They are hornless, generally dun in colour, and have round ears. If a water-bull comes and mates with one of a herd of earthly cattle it is thought to be a great improvement to the stock, but if a water-cow joins an earthly herd she has to be watched carefully, for at night she will make for a fairy hill, which will open for her, and if the cow-herd does not turn back the rest of the cattle they will follow her into the hill and be kept there. There is a story about a farmer in Islay who had a large herd of cattle and a little bull-calf which had round ears was born to one of the cows. An old woman who lived on the farm and whose advice was always taken said at once that this was the calf of a water-bull. She told the farmer to keep it separate from the other calves for three years and to feed it every day with the milk of three cows. This they did, and it grew into a splendid bull. One day when the farmer's lassie was down by the sea-loch watching the herd a young man came up and sat down beside her. They talked for a while very pleasantly and then he asked her to clean his head. It was a thing lassies often did for their lads in those days. So he lay down and put his head on her lap and she began to part and straighten his hair. As she did this she saw with horror that there was green seaweed growing amongst his hair, and she knew he must be the dreadful each uisge, the water-horse, but she had a brave heart; she did not start or scream. She went steadily and gently on with her task and began to sing a little crooning song, so that the disguised monster was lulled to sleep. Then, very carefully and stealthily, she untied her apron and edged herself away from under it, leaving the each uisge asleep on the ground, and ran away towards the farm as silently as she could. She had almost reached it when she heard a great thunder of hoofs behind her, and there was the fierce water-horse hard on her heels. Then she screamed and screamed. A moment and she would have been carried into the loch and torn in pieces; but the old woman had heard her, and she loosed the crodh mara, which came trumpeting out and attacked the each uisge. The two went fighting down into the loch together and disappeared into the deep water. Next morning the body of the crodh mara was washed up, but the each uisge was never seen again.

Cu Sith *(coo-shee)*. The cu sith, the fairy dog of the Highlands, was unlike the ordinary fairy hounds, who were white with red ears. It was dark green, the size of a two-year-old stirk (yearling bullock) and shaggy, with a long tail coiled up on its back. Its feet were enormous, as broad as a man's, and its great footmarks were often seen in mud or snow, but it glided along silently, moving in a straight line. It did not bark or yap when hunting, but gave three tremendous bays which could be heard by ships far out at sea. Most of the fairy dogs were kept tied up inside the brugh, or fairy house, to be loosed against intruders, or were taken out by the fairy women, but the cu sith was sometimes allowed to roam out alone and then it would be terribly dangerous to mortal men or dogs.

The commonest fairy dogs in England are the BLACK DOGS which are solitary and independent, but there are packs of black dogs, the DEVIL'S DANDY DOGS, the GABRIEL HOUNDS and others, which are directed by a supernatural huntsman.

Dando and His Dogs. Dando was a wicked priest who cared for nothing so much as hunting, though he loved drinking and revelry too. Sundays and weekdays were the same to him, and one fine Sunday Dando and his rout were out hunting over an estate near by called Earth. They had had magnificent sport and made many kills, but when they paused to bait their horses Dando found that there was no drink left in the flasks of any of his attendants. He was furiously thirsty, and he shouted out, "If you can't find any decent drink on Earth, go to Hell for it." At that a stranger who had joined the hunt rode up and offered Dando his flask. "I think you'll find this drink to your taste," he said. "It comes from the place you mentioned."

Dando tasted it and emptied the whole flask, and it was a big one. He smacked his lips and swore a dreadful oath. "If they have drink like this in Hell," he said, "I'd willingly spend Eternity there."

Just then he noticed that the stranger was quietly collecting all the game that had been caught. "Here," he shouted, "Leave that alone! That's mine." "What I have I hold," said the stranger, and slung the game over the back of his great black horse. "I'll follow you to Hell for it!" said Dando, and, flinging himself off his horse, he rushed to the stranger's side and began to drum him with his fists.

"You *shall* go with me to Hell for it!" said the stranger, and, picking up Dando by the scruff of his neck, he set him in front of

him on the great horse and spurred into the deepest part of the river. A spurt of flame went up and the horse with its two riders disappeared; but we cannot imagine Dando sitting quietly drinking in Hell, for on stormy nights he is heard in full chase over the countryside with his hounds before him.

Danes. There is some confusion among the people of Somerset between the Danes who raided the countryside a thousand years ago and the fairies, the "dana", as the Celtic people called them. Ruth Tongue was once told by a man living near Dolbury Camp about the treasure that was supposed to be buried by the Danes; but according to him the Danes were the fairies.

There be a bit of verse do go

> If Dolbury digged were
> Of gold should be the share,

but nobody hasn't found the treasure yet. And for why? Well, to start up with it don't belong to they, and so they won't never meet up with it. 'Twill go on sinking down below, never mind how deep they do dig.

I tell 'ee 'tis the gold of they Redshanks as used to be seed on Dolbury top. To be sure there's clever, book-read gentlemen as tell as they was Danes, and another say 'twere all on account of their bare legs being red with the wind; but don't mind they.

My granny she did tell they was fairies, ah, and all dressed in red, and if so the treasure must be theirs. If they was Danes how do 'ee explain all they little clay pipes as 'ee can find on Dolbury Camp. They did call 'em "fairy pipes", old miners did. An' if there be fairy pipes then there was fairies, and nobody need doubt they was the Redshanks.

And that's what the country people round Dolbury still believe.

Daoine Sidhe *(theena shee)*. The Daoine Sidhe are the regular fairy people of Ireland. They were once tall and beautiful, almost like gods, but they have gradually dwindled down until they are now sometimes called "the Little People" or "the Wee Folks". But people are still frightened of them and they do not often call them "the Deeny Shee", but instead "the Gentry", "the Good People", "the People of That Town", for it is unlucky to call them by their real name. They were once the real heroic fairies, who lived like the knights of olden days, riding, hunting, dancing, great lovers of music and song, and always busy over feuds and

faction fights. Even in modern times they are not always tiny, but are sometimes described as of human size, or more. Their houses are either underground or under water – under the green knolls or beneath the lakes, or under the sea. Sometimes fishermen out at night say they see a moving line of lights shining up from the bottom of the sea. They are the Good People travelling home to their palaces under the waves.

Devil's Dandy Dogs. There are many names for the Wild Hunt in different parts of England and they differ from place to place, but the most dangerous to living men are the Devil's Dandy Dogs of Cornwall. Some of the other Wild Hunts chase witches and some lost souls, and in Scandinavia the poor little elf-women are the quarry. But it is lonely travellers belated on the wild moors of Cornwall who are the prey of the Devil's Dandy Dogs. There is a defence against them; anyone who is brave enough to stop running

and kneel down to pray is safe, but it takes a brave heart to do it.

A poor herdsman was once travelling home on a dark windy night across the moors when he heard in the distance the baying of hounds. It was too late for a mortal pack to be out, and as it came nearer he made out that it was the Devil's Dandy Dogs. He started to run as fast as he could across the rough ground, for his home was still a good four miles away, but the baying and the wild hoot of the huntsman's horn came nearer and nearer. At last as he glanced over his shoulder he saw lights dancing nearer, and soon he could make out the shapes of the black hounds with fiery eyes and horns on their heads, and their dreadful rider, on a black horse with flames coming from its eyes and mouth. He knew no running could help him, so he fell on his knees. At least he would die praying. The pack was almost on him when the huntsman gave a shrill whistle. "Bo shrove," he cried, which is the Cornish for "The boy prays", and the pack drew back whining, with their tails between their legs. The huntsman turned his horse aside and whistled again. The whole pack wheeled round, and away they went at full speed, hunting for less Christian souls. The herdsman finished his prayers and made his way home, full of thankfulness.

Dobby. Dobby is a friendly name for a HOBGOBLIN in Yorkshire and Lancashire. He is very like a BROWNIE but perhaps more

likely to play pranks. In Sussex there was a brownie called Dobbs
or Master Dobbs, who was particularly kind to old men. He was
very like the Yorkshire dobby.

Dooinney-Oie or "Night-Man". This is a kindly spirit who gives
warnings of storms, sometimes by a voice shouting, sometimes by
the misty appearance of a man who speaks and gives warning,

and sometimes by the blowing of a horn which sounds rather like
a Swiss alpen-horn. The Howlaa is another creature which gives
warnings of storms in the Isle of Man, but it only does it by
howling, it does not show itself or speak. Dora Broome tells an
amusing story in *Fairy Tales from the Isle of Man* about a
dooinney-oie who got too fond of playing his horn.

Doonie. The Doonie is the Scottish version of the Northumberland DUNNIE but it is kinder. Like the Dunnie it can take the form of a pony, or of a man or woman. It does not play tricks or mislead, like the Dunnie; all the stories told of it are of rescue or guiding. There is one told about 1903 of a schoolboy who was rescued by the Doonie.

This boy was climbing the steep rock which overhangs Crichope Linn in Dumfriesshire to take young rock-doves out of their nests, when his foot slipped and he fell right down the precipice. He managed to catch hold of a hazel bush but it was too small to hold him for more than a few minutes. He looked down to see if he would be drowned in the Linn or dashed to pieces on the rocks, and saw a strange old woman standing on a ledge below him and holding out her apron. She called to him to jump into it, and he jumped – there was no other choice. The apron gave way and he fell into the Linn. The old woman pulled him out by the scruff of his neck, and led him up to the top by a hidden way that he could never find again, however much he looked for it. Then she told him to get home and to leave the doves alone in the future. "Or maybe," she said, "the Doonie'll be no here tae kep ye." And with that she was gone.

Dragons. St George's dragon was like dragons we see in heraldry and in many pictures. He had bat's wings, a sting in his tail and a fiery breath; but many of the English dragons are like the Scandinavian worms, very long, wingless and with poisonous breath. They are so long that they can coil several times round a hill, and there are various places in England called Wormshill, as well as some man-made mounds round which the worms used to curl, like the hill round which the Linton Worm, who was killed by the "Wode Laird of Lariston", used to curl himself when he had finished ravaging the countryside. The Laird of Lariston killed him by thrusting a burning peat down his throat, which is an effective way of killing worms. The largest worm of all, the Meister Stoorworm of Orkney, was killed in this way. His liver caught fire, his teeth shot out and became the scattered islands round Shetland, and his curled-up body became Iceland. He died hundreds of years ago, but his huge liver is still burning and that is what causes the volcanoes in Iceland.

Both kinds of dragons are covered with scales and have great claws, both are treasure-guards, and both are much interested in maidens. The heraldic dragons are small in comparison with the worms, in fact the one in Carpaccio's picture of St George and the Dragon is so small that one is quite sorry for the little thing. But even the smallest were very dangerous.

The Dragon of Wantley was much larger than Carpaccio's dragon. This dragon was the terror of the countryside. He had forty-four iron teeth in his jaw, great wings, a long sting in his tail and a fiery breath. He ate trees and cattle and children, and because of his breath no man dared to come near him. Quite close to the dragon's den there lived a fierce, wild knight called More of More Hall, who was as strong as a giant and had a hot temper. He was afraid of nothing, so at last the people came to him and begged him to rid them of the dragon. They offered him all the money they had left if he killed the dragon, but he said he would do it for nothing if they would lend him a black-haired maiden of sixteen to anoint him all over on the night before the battle and to dress him in his armour in the morning. When they promised this he went to a blacksmith and had a suit of armour made for him covered all over with iron spikes. When this was ready and the maiden had buckled him into it, he went and hid early in the morning in the spring where the dragon used to come down to drink. When it poked its head into the spring, More jumped up with a great shout and hit it on the snout with his mailed fist. A tremendous fight started which lasted for two days and two nights, but neither could break through the other's guard. At length the dragon swooped back and made a dash forward to seize More and lift him up into the air, but More stepped aside, and as the dragon rushed past him he brought his spiked heel down on the monster's back. He had reached the dragon's weak spot. It curled itself up and spun round and round until it dropped down dead. And that was the end of the Dragon of Wantley.

This one unprotected spot on the dragon's body is a part of the dragon tradition. You will perhaps remember how Smaug, the dragon in *The Hobbit* by J. R. R. Tolkien, was shot through the one spot on his huge body not protected by coins. Professor Tolkien knew a great deal about dragons.

Duergar. Duergars are the black dwarfs of the North of England, always full of malice towards men and eager to destroy them. They say a foot traveller was once crossing the Simonside Hills in Northumberland on his way to Rothbury. Darkness came down, and he lost the path. He knew that if he went on he might at any moment tumble down a precipice, but if he sat down in the bitter cold he would freeze to death. So he groped on very slowly, looking for some kind of shelter. Presently he saw a faint light in front of him and after a time he saw that it came from a smouldering fire inside a little rough stone hut, such as the shepherds build for shelter in the lambing time. The traveller went in thankfully and in the dim light made out that he was in a stone hut, almost a cave, with two big stones as seats, one on each side of the fire, a pile of kindling to the left of it and two heavy logs to the right. He revived the fire with some of the kindling and sat down on the right-hand stone to warm his numbed hands and feet.

He had hardly sat down before the door was flung open and a strange figure came in. He was a little dwarf, only as high as the traveller's knee, but broad and strong in proportion. He wore a lambskin coat, his breeches and shoes were of moleskins and he had a hat of green moss with a pheasant's feather in it. He said nothing, but scowled at the traveller, stamped over to the left-hand

stone and perched on it. The traveller said nothing either, for he was sure that his host was a duergar, and he knew how bitterly they hate mankind. So they sat opposite each other in silence; the fire died down and the hut got colder and colder. Presently the traveller could bear it no longer, so he picked up some of the kindling and revived the fire. The dwarf looked furiously at him, but still said nothing. After a time he seemed to be making signs to his guest to put on one of the great logs, but the traveller did nothing. At length the dwarf bent back and picked up one of the great logs. It was twice as long as he was and thicker than his body, but he broke it across his knee and fed the fire with the pieces. It blazed up, but soon died down again. The dwarf made

63

motions to the man as much as to say, "Why can't you do like me?" but the man thought there was some catch in it, and sat on, though the cold was bitter.

At length a faint light began to show through the chinks, and far away a cock crowed. At the sound the duergar disappeared and the hut and the fire with him. The traveller was still sitting on his stone, but it was the topmost peak of a great crag at the top of a ravine. If he had moved only a few inches to the right to pick up the log he would have slid into the ravine, and nothing would have been left of him but broken bones.

Dunnie. There only seems to have been one Dunnie, who haunted the district of Hazelrigg on Belford Moor. He behaved just like the BRAG or the HEDLEY KOW, but he was supposed to be the ghost of a Border reiver who had a great treasure hidden in one of the caves on a crag called Bowden Doors, and who was killed on one of his raids before he could tell anyone where it was hidden. This is said to be a great cause of haunting. The Dunnie used to be heard saying a mournful rhyme about it:

> "Cocken heugh there's gear enough,
>   Collier heugh there's mair,
> For I've lost the key o' the Bounders,
>   An' I'm ruined for evermair."

But when he was not lamenting he was busy playing practical jokes, like any ordinary bogey-beast. Sometimes he took the form of a donkey, but one of his favourite tricks was to pretend to be the farmer's plough-horse and to allow himself to be led out to the field and fastened to the plough. Then suddenly the harness would all fall to the ground and he would be seen galloping and plunging away into the distance. Or he would allow the farmer to mount him to fetch the midwife, and bring her to her patient safely enough, but on the way back, when her work was done, he would suddenly disappear at the ford and leave the farmer and the mid-wife to get out of the river as best they could. He had all kinds of tricks that he played, but he must have been laid long ago, for no one has heard of him for more than a hundred years.

Dunters. The dunters were Border spirits who used to haunt old peel towers and Border keeps. They were not as wicked as the REDCAPS, but they made a constant noise, like beating flax or grinding barley in a hollow stone quern. In the northern counties they say that if the sound gets louder it is an omen of death or misfortune.

It used to be said too that these peel towers were built by the Picts and had been sprinkled with blood as a foundation sacrifice. The suggestion is that dunters and redcaps were the spirits of the creatures which had been sacrificed.

Dwarfs. The Dwarfs are more common in Germany, Switzerland and the Isle of Rügen than in the British Isles, and though there are many small fairies that might be called dwarfs they generally have names of their own. The Cornish mine spirits are called KNOCKERS, BLUE-CAPS and dunters, who make as much noise as the Border DUNTERS do. The fairies who visited KING HERLA were dwarfs but they were described as satyrs. Some of the solitary

65

fairies like the DUERGARS are called dwarfs, and the "wee, wee man" in the ballad is a dwarf, though he is not called one. The mysterious ladies who met King Arthur's knights often had a dwarf with them, but it is doubtful whether these were fairies or dwarfed humans like those who were kept as jesters in royal courts in later times. The little industrious dwarfs who lived in cottages and went to quarry jewels and gold in the mines, like those who adopted Snow White, are not to be found in these islands.

1. A fairy bride, a goddess who has fallen in love with a mortal man.
2. Mermaids, beautiful maidens with long golden hair who have the body and tail of a fish instead of human legs.
3. Waiting for the Queen of the Seelie Court to change her lover back into a man.
4. Changelings left to take the place of human babies or of nursing mothers stolen by the fairies.
5. The leprachaun, a fairy shoemaker, who is supposed to have won great wealth which he will yield up if he is caught.
6. St. George and the Dragon.
7. Finvarra, the Fairy King of Ulster, often said to be the King of the Dead as well.
8. Nuckelavee, an Orkney sea-monster like a horrible centaur.
9. Peg O'Nell, who died and became the evil spirit of the river Ribble in Lancashire.
10. The Lady of the Lake, a water fairy who stole the baby Lancelot and carried him away to a magic island.

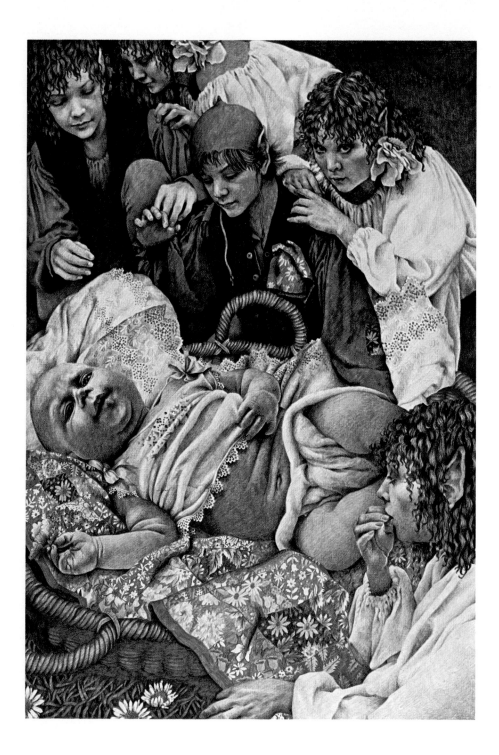

Each Uisge *(agh-iski)*. The water-horses are all fierce and danger-ous, but the Highland each uisge is the worst of all, though the Manx cabyll-ushtey runs it close. It differs from the kelpie in haunting the sea and sea lochs, while kelpies belong to running water, though occasionally we have a water-horse story told of a fresh-water loch. The each uisge seems to change its shape more often than a kelpie. Its usual form is that of a sleek and handsome horse, which almost offers itself to be ridden, but if anyone is so rash as to mount it he is carried at headlong speed into the water and devoured. Only his liver is uneaten, and it floats to shore. It is said that its skin is sticky and the rider cannot tear himself off it. It also appears sometimes as a huge bird and sometimes as a handsome young man.

There are a great many legends of each uisge in his horse form. One that seems as if it had been told as a warning is about a small lochan near Aberfeldy in Perthshire. Seven little girls and a little boy were going for a walk together one Sunday afternoon when they saw a pretty little pony grazing near the loch. The eldest little girl scrambled on to the pony's back and called a friend to join her, and one by one each little girl scrambled up. There seemed plenty of room for them all, and the little boy, who was a more cautious type than the girls, noticed that the pony grew a little longer as each girl got on its back. There were some boulders near the loch, and he hid among them. Suddenly the pony turned its head and noticed him. It yelled in a human voice, "Come here little scabby-head and get on my back!" but the boy darted further in among the rocks. The little girls all screamed together and tried to jump off, but their hands seemed glued to the pony's back as he darted in and out among the stones, trying to catch the little boy. At length he gave it up and plunged into the loch with the girls on his back. Next morning the livers of the seven children were washed up on the shore. There are many stories like this told about the water-horse, though in some the victim escapes as, for example, in the story of the CRODH MARA and the water-horse.

Ellyllon *(ethlerthlon)*. This is the name given to the Welsh elves. They are tiny, elegant fairies, whose food is toadstools and "fairy butter", which is a little yellow fungus found in the roots of old trees. Their queen is Mab, and they are smaller than the TYLWETH TEG.

In one story, from Peterstone near Cardiff, they seem more like ordinary trooping fairies, the "Good People", who are sorry for humans in misfortune. There was a poor farmer called Rowli Pugh who seemed to be always unlucky. If blight came anywhere it fell on his crops; when every other farmer had healthy cattle, his were sick. His wife was an invalid who had no strength to do anything about the farm, and Rowli was thinking one day that he would have to sell it and go when he met a little ellyl who spoke to him kindly. "Don't you trouble yourself any more," he said. "We'll look after you. Tell Catti, your wife, to sweep the floor clean every night, leave a bright fire and a lighted candle, and go early to bed. We'll do the rest." Rowli believed him and hurried home to tell Catti, who set to and swept the room with a good will. The ellyl was as good as his word. Every night Rowli and Catti went early to bed and left the house clean for the Ellyllon. Every night they heard laughter, merriment and bustle beneath them. In the morning everything was in apple-pie order. The cattle were fed and cleaned, the crops were tended, and Catti and Rowli grew sleek, strong and merry, without a care in the world. And so three years passed prosperously. But Catti began to long to see the merry little people. One night she left her husband fast asleep in bed, tiptoed downstairs and peeped through a crack in the door. There were the elves, working, singing, laughing and playing pranks all at the same time. They were so merry and comical that Catti burst out laughing too. At once there was a cry and a scampering; the candle was blown out and the Ellyllon left Pugh's Farm for ever. But, unlike many fairies, they took no revenge for being spied on. Rowli had learned the elves' neat, orderly ways, Catti was well and active, and the farm went on prospering.

Elves. In Scandinavia in olden days the fairy people were called elves, and were divided into light elves and dark elves, like the Scottish SEELIE COURT and UNSEELIE COURT. The name came over into Britain with the Saxons, and in the Anglo-Saxon medical books we find remedies against elf-shot and other dangerous elvish practices. The mythological light-elves were not unlike the trooping fairies of England as we find them in *A Midsummer Night's Dream* and many English fairy stories. In Christian times the Scandinavians went on believing in the elves, or *huldre folk* (the "hidden people"), who were much the same as the Scottish fairies, both Highland and Lowland. They stole humans away, milked cattle, and avenged themselves for any injuries or insults. The *huldre* girls were beautiful and alluring, wearing grey dresses and white veils, but, like other fairies, they could be recognized by a defect – they had long cows' tails. A man who was dancing with a *huldre* girl saw her tail and realized what she was, but he did

not betray her. He said, "Pretty maid, you are losing your garter." His tact was rewarded by good luck all his life. The defect of the Danish elves, or "ellewomen", was different. They were beautiful from the front, but they were hollow behind, like a rotten tree. Because of this they never turned round in their dances.

In Lowland Scotland and in England the word "elves" had slightly different meanings. In Scotland the fairy people of human size were often called elves, and Fairyland was Elfame; in England it was the smaller trooping fairies who were called elves, and the name was specially used for small fairy boys. "Elf", however, was as unpopular with the fairies themselves as the tactless name of "fairy" – that is, if we can judge from the rhyme given by R. Chambers in his *Popular Rhymes of Scotland*:

> Gin ye ca' me imp or elf,
> I rede ye look weel to yourself;
> Gin ye ca' me fairy,
> I'll work ye muckle tarrie;
> Gin guid neibour ye ca' me,
> Then guid neibour I will be;
> But gin ye ca' me seelie wicht,
> I'll be your freend baith day and nicht.

"Fairies on the Eastern Green". This story of a meeting between the fairies and the smugglers is about Zennor in Cornwall, and it was told by an innkeeper there at the end of the last century.

Tom Warren of Paul was one of the boldest of the smugglers anywhere round about. On a summer night about forty years back he and five other men landed a cargo of smuggled goods not far from Long Rock. When the brandy, salt and silks had been taken above high-water mark, two of the men set out for Market-Jew, where their best customers lived, and one went into Norton to fetch horses, so that the goods might be taken into hiding before daylight.

Tom and the other two, being very tired, lay down by the heap of goods, hoping to get a doze whilst their comrades were away; but they were soon waked by the shrill tweeting of feapers (those are slit quills or reeds, which give a shrill tootle when they are blown). Besides there was a shrill tinkling, just like old women make by rattling pewter plates together to make their swarming bees settle.

The men thought this noise might be from a company of young folks keeping up a dance on the Green till a very late hour. Tom went to see who they were and to send them home, for it didn't do to have everybody prying into the Fair Traders' business. He crossed the beach and climbed a high sandbank to have a look round, as the music sounded very near. At a little distance, in hollows between sand-banks, he saw glimmering lights, and little people, like gaily dressed dolls, skipping about and whirling round.

Going nearer he could see, perched on a pretty high bank in their midst, about twenty little old-looking chaps; many of them blew mouth-organs, some had cymbals or tambourines, and others played on jew's harps, or tweeted on May whistles and feapers.

Tom noticed that the little men were rigged out all in green, except for their scarlet caps. But what struck him and tickled his fancy most was to see the little, old, grave-looking pipers with their long beards wagging. In moving their mouths over the reeds stuck against their chests they looked more like billy-goats than anything human – so Tom said, and that for the life of him he couldn't help shouting – "Will 'ee be shaved, old red-caps?" He hailed them twice, and was just going to do so again, when all the dancers, with scores and hundreds more than he had noticed at first, armed themselves with bows and arrows and spears and advanced towards him, looking like vengeance. The band ranged themselves alongside and played a quick march, and the troops of SPRIGGANS stamped up towards Tom, who saw them getting

73

taller and taller as they came nearer. Their threatening looks were so frightful that he ran down to his comrades and woke them up, saying: "Put to sea for your lives! There's thousands of small people and bucca-boos 'most on our backs! They'll soon surround us!" With that Tom made off to his boat, and his companions followed close on his heels, but on the way a shower of pebbles fell on them, and "burned like coals o' fire wherever they hit 'em".

The men pulled many fathoms away from the shore before they dared to look up, though they really knew themselves safe on the sea, because none of the fairy tribe dared touch salt water.

At length they cast a glance landward and saw, ranged up along the shore, a company of as ugly-looking creatures as they had ever beheld, making threatening gestures at them and slinging a shower of stones which all fell short. When they were about a furlong from land the men rested on their oars and kept watching their enemies till it was near daybreak. Then they heard the horses galloping along the road from Market-Jew. At the sound the small people made off, and the smugglers judged it was safe to row back to land.

The smugglers collected their gear, and were not attacked again by spriggans or bucca-boos, but it is said that bad luck followed Tom after this adventure. It is clear that the fairies do not like being watched any more than the smugglers do, and they are always very angry if anyone mocks them.

Fairy Animals. There are a great many fairy animals all over the British Isles, but they are on the whole of two kinds. First there are the wild fairy animals that belong to themselves and have no masters, and second there are the animals trained and used by the Fairies, the domestic animals that serve the fairy people. Both kinds come very early in our traditions and are to be found in the medieval chronicles. The Grant, for instance, is a wild fairy animal, a kind of bogey-beast, and the little fairy dogs and horses used by the good little fairies who were so kind to the boy Elidor are the fairy domestic animals. I mention both of these in my Introduction.

Examples of the wild fairy horses are the terrible EACH UISGE of the Highlands, the kelpies, the CABYLL-USHTEY of the Isle of

Man, and such BOGIES as the BRAG and the SHOCK. All these have some power of shape-shifting. The horses used by the fairies are to be found everywhere in the heroic fairy legends, wherever there is a fairy rade. (A rade was the old name for a solemn procession on horseback.) The BLACK DOGS are the most widespread of the free fairy dogs, but there are other bogey-beast dogs, the BARGUEST and the padfoot, and the Suffolk SHOCK sometimes takes the form of a dog. The CU SITH are the dogs of the PEOPLE OF PEACE in the Highlands.

The wild fairy cattle, the CRODH MARA of the Highlands and the taroo-ushtey of the Isle of Man, are less dangerous than the water-horses, and the fairy domestic cattle, like those brought by the FAIRY BRIDES as dowry, are welcome additions to any herds.

Of the many different creatures the most famous were the seal people. Cats were almost fairies in themselves, but there was a fairy cat in the Highlands, the *cait sith*, which was dark green, and a demon-god cat, Big Ears, which appeared after horrible invocations.

The Afanc was a river monster of Wales, something like a giant beaver, and in the Highlands of Scotland there was a gigantic bird called the boobrie, with a voice to match. Many birds, particularly the owl, the eagle, the raven, the robin and the wren, had strong fairy associations and the Cornish chough was until quite lately supposed to be the reincarnation of King Arthur. Certain trout and salmon were supposed in Ireland to be fairy creatures. Even insects had their part. The Gooseberry Wife appeared in the form of a large hairy caterpillar. In fact all of these islands are rich in fairy zoology.

Fairy Brides. There were many legends told in Ancient Greece and Rome of how nymphs and goddesses visited mortal men and fell in love with them, but these loves usually ended in tragedy because the goddesses were immortal and the men were born to die.

The same kind of stories were told about the fairies long after people had ceased to believe in the goddesses.

The churchmen and the monks who lived in the Middle Ages were the people who wrote history in the old days because they had been trained to read and write. They told quite a lot of fairy anecdotes in their chronicles, and several of these are about fairy wives. One chronicler, Walter Map, first tells us the famous story of WILD EDRIC, which was handed down by word of mouth in Shropshire till the nineteenth century.

Map has another story, "The Fairy Wife of Brecknock Mere". He tells that Gwestin of Gwestiniog on three brilliant moonlight nights saw bands of beautiful women dancing in one of his fields of oats, and followed them until they disappeared under the waters of Brecknock Mere. He fell in love with one of them, and tried to capture her, and it seemed that she rather wanted to be caught, for every night he heard her murmuring under the water, "If he had only done so-and-so he would have caught me." So the third night he did just as she had said and she consented to be his wife, but she said that if he ever struck her with his bridle-rein she must leave him. They lived very happily together for years, and had many children, but one day it happened that as she was helping him to catch his horse to go off to the Border Riding he threw the

bridle to her, and the bit accidentally touched her. He hardly noticed it, and went off to the Riding, but as he came back he saw her leaving the farm with all her children. He followed her at once, and with great difficulty succeeded in snatching back one son, Trinio Faglog, from the cavalcade. It is strange that there is someone still alive who traces her descent from this fairy lady.

In modern Welsh tradition there are several stories of fairy brides, and one of them, "The Fairy of Fan y Fach", is very like Walter Map's story, written down nearly six hundred years earlier. In this one the bride is courted with bread and cheese thrown into the lake. She is very particular about the way it is baked, but at the third try he gets it right and she rises out of the lake with her father, who gives her a splendid dowry of cattle, but says that she is never to be struck, and if her husband strikes her three times she will leave him for ever and take all her cattle with her. In the end this happens, and the husband and his sons are left alone. But the sons had the gift of healing from their fairy mother and they became the famous Physicians of Midvai.

There is another story of a fairy bridal which had a happier end. It is a thirteenth-century poem called "The Romance of Sir Launfal". Queen Guinevere is the villainess of this poem. Sir Launfal disapproves of her marriage to Arthur and leaves the court. While he is living in Caerleon, poor and alone, a maiden comes to invite him to visit the fairy Lady Tryamour. Tryamour is very beautiful and Launfal falls deeply in love with her. She gives him all kinds of beautiful things, clothes and weapons and servants and a wonderful horse and a bottomless purse. She will be with him whenever he wishes for her, invisible to everyone else, but there is one condition – their love is a secret, he must never boast of her nor tell who gave him his gifts, or he will lose her.

They were very happy together and he performed great feats of arms, so that King Arthur heard of them and summoned him back to court. Still Lady Tryamour came to him invisibly, and they were still happy, but Queen Guinevere was very angry that Sir Launfal would have nothing to do with her, and she taunted and sneered at him until one day he lost his temper and said that he had a lady whose meanest serving-maid was more beautiful than Queen

Guinevere or any of her ladies. When he went to see his lady she had gone, and so was his horse and his armour and all his rich clothing, and his bottomless purse was empty.

While Sir Launfal was distracted with grief Queen Guinevere brought a wicked accusation against him, and he was brought to trial. But many of the knights of the court knew that Queen Guinevere was a bad woman, and they asked for a further trial and said that since Sir Launfal had spoken disdainfully of the queen and her court he must be allowed time to make good his words and produce his beautiful lady. Sir Launfal had no hope, for he knew that he had forfeited his lady by his boasting, and Queen Guinevere became more exultant as the days went by. At length it was the last day; the gallows were set up and Sir Launfal brought out to die. But the knights said, "The day is not yet over, we must wait till the sunset." So they waited, and when the sun was getting low ten ladies in rich clothes came riding into the field. And the knights said, "It is true; they are all more beautiful than any of our ladies. Which of them is your bride, Launfal?" And Launfal said, "None of these is my lady." Then another ten, still more beautiful, rode in, and still Sir Launfal said that none of these was his lady. Then at last one lady on a white horse rode through the town, Lady Tryamour, shining like a star, and Sir Launfal said, "This is my Lady." And the knights and the ladies cried out that he had spoken no more than the truth. At that Sir Launfal's horse was led by his squire out of the wood, and he mounted and rode off with his lady, and the whole bevy of ladies followed them, and they all rode off to the Isle of Olyroun in Fairyland. Sir Launfal has never been seen again by mortal man, but once a year, on a certain day, his horse is heard neighing in Fairyland and a bugle sounds a challenge, and if any man were bold enough to answer it Launfal would come out to joust with him.

The fairies used always to forbid people to tell of their gifts, and this tradition lasted till the nineteenth century.

In the Irish traditions there are stories of fairies who took their mortal lovers to live with them on enchanted islands. The most famous of these is OISIN, the son of Fion of the Fianna Finn, who returned to see his country after many hundreds of years had passed and had to remain in the mortal world because his foot had touched the soil of Ireland.

Bran, the son of Febal, was more fortunate. He was warned by the fate of one of his comrades, who leapt ashore and crumbled to dust. He did not get out of his boat, but told his adventures to the people who had gathered round, then turned her head to sea again and went back to his fairy island.

The SELKIES, or seal people, are another set of fairy wives. They need their sealskins to go through the sea, and when these are stolen they are imprisoned on the land; but it always seems to happen that in the end they find their skins and go back to their selkie husbands.

Fenoderee. There are about five ways of spelling the name of this creature, which is generally called the "Manx Brownie". He behaves very like a BROWNIE, though he looks more like an URISK. He is large and hairy and ugly, and enormously strong. There is a story about how when the Fenoderee was working in Gordon he happened to meet the blacksmith one night and offered to shake hands with him. The blacksmith had the good sense to hold out the share of a plough which he was carrying, and Fenoderee gripped it so hard that he twisted it almost out of shape, saying approvingly, "I'm glad to see there's still some strong Manxmen left in the world yet."

Rough and strong though he was, the Fenoderee was supposed to have been one of the FERRISHYN, the small trooping fairies of Man. He had fallen in love with a mortal girl and had been dancing with her in Glen Rushen when he should have been at the fairies' autumn festival. For this he had been given a hairy shape and banished from Fairyland till the Day of Judgement. In spite of what he had suffered because of them he still loved mortals, and he worked all over the Island, at one farm or another, at a furious rate. Like an ordinary brownie, he could be touchy; once a farmer hurt his feelings by saying that he did not crop the grass close enough, so he followed the farmer closely, grubbing up the roots with his sharp tool until the farmer was afraid of having his heels cut off.

Like a brownie, too, he expected his supply of food, but did not want any other reward. Once he had done a tremendous work carrying hewed stones from the beach to build a house at Sholt-e-Will, and the owner wanted to show his gratitude and left him out a complete set of new clothes. The servants hid and listened. Fenoderee picked up the clothes one by one and chanted:

> "Cap for the head, alas poor head!
> Coat for the back, alas poor back!
> Breeches for the breech, alas poor breech!
> If these be all thine, thine cannot be
>   the merry Glen of Rusen!"

And with that he went wailing away.

Ferrishyn. This is one of the Manx names for the fairy tribe. The Ferrishyn are the small, trooping fairies of the Isle of Man. They are not so grand as the fairies of Ireland and Wales, for they have no named king or queen. They are small, generally about three feet in height, though some people say they only measure one foot high. They steal human babies and leave changelings behind, like other fairies, and they love to visit human houses at night, when everyone has gone to bed, and to use human workshops for their crafts. Their favourite sport is hunting, and the fairy hunt must be a gay sight, for the fairy huntsmen wear green coats and red caps. The hounds are sometimes said to be white with red ears, like other fairy dogs, but some people who claimed to have seen the hunt said that the hounds were of all the colours of the rainbow – red, blue, green and yellow.

In old days, when many people believed in the fairies, men used to be very careful how they spoke of the Ferrishyn out of doors, for they believed that every breath of wind carried the spoken words to their ears, and it was very unlucky to offend them.

Finvarra. Finvarra is the Fairy King of Ulster, but he is often said to be the King of the Dead as well. In a story called "November Eve" we are told how a fisherman, Hugh King, who rashly returned home late from the fishing on Halloween night, blundered into a fairy fair and found, as he looked at them, that all the dancers were dead men whom he had known. Finvarra and his wife drove up to the fair in a coach drawn by four white horses. "Out of it stepped a grand, grave gentleman all in black and a beautiful lady with a silver veil over her face." In another story, "Ethna the Bride", we see Finvarra as the thief of beautiful human women, just as Pluto carried off Persephone. There is another story of Finvarra as a horseman on a black horse lending one of the Kirwans of Galway a jockey who won a great race for him. After it Finvarra took young Kirwan to dinner in a grand castle – probably Knockma, Finvarra's fairy mound – where he gradually recognized the splendid company as the dead whom he had known when they were alive. Though he ate the banquet and drank the fairy wine he came to less harm than most mortals who eat and drink in Fairyland. But he came back with a burnt ring round his wrist left by the hand of a girl whom he had loved in old days and who had died before they were married, and this burnt ring never healed.

Foul-Weather. Foul-Weather is the name of the Cornish Tom Tit Tot or Whuppity Stoorie, only this story is about the building of a great church.

There was once a king of a far country who had set his heart on building the most beautiful cathedral in his whole kingdom. He had it all planned, but by the time the foundations were laid he had spent all the money in his coffers. He could think of no way of finishing it except by laying heavy taxes on his people, and he did not think it would be right to do this. One day he went out alone in the mountains, trying to make up his mind what he ought to do, and there he met a strange old man. "Why art thou so deep in thought?" said the strange man. "Why should I not be deep in thought," said the king, "when I have begun a great cathedral, and have not the money to finish it." "Never trouble thy head about that," said the old man. "I myself will build thee a fair cathedral, better than any in thy realm, and I will not ask a penny of money for it." "What wilt thou ask for it then?" said the king, who was no fool. "King, if you can call me by my name before the church is finished," said the dwarf, "it is yours for nothing, but if you cannot guess it I will take your heart in payment."

The king knew then that the strange man was one of the wicked GOBLINS of the Mountains, but he thought the building would take a long, long time, so that he might be dead by the time it was finished, and if he was dead he would not mind what happened to his heart. So he said, "I agree," and the goblin vanished.

During the day nothing happened, but that night there was a tremendous racket round the place where the foundations of the cathedral lay, and swarms of goblinish creatures came round it carrying great stones as if they were as light as corks, and next

morning the great thick walls of the cathedral were three feet high all round. The king thought and thought of names to call the goblin, and every night he tried a fresh one, but all the goblin builders yelled with laughter and told him to try again. So he began to think of fresh improvements to make so as to slow down the work, but everything he suggested was done in a single night.

And now the high spire began to rise. So that day he went up into the mountain to think of any fresh adornment that could be made. He wandered up and into the mountains until, as the sun was getting low in the sky, he came to the mouth of a deep cave, and a terrible squalling was coming out of it, such as a hundred mortal babies could not make. It was a goblin baby squalling its head off. Presently there were thunderous footsteps inside the cave, and then he could hear from the cries that the baby was picked up and rocked to and fro, while a hoarse, harsh voice droned out:

> "Weep not, weep not, my darling boy;
> Hush altogether
> And then Foul-Weather,
> Thy dad, will come
> Tomorrow home,
> Bringing a king's heart for thy joy
> To play withal, a pretty toy."

Loudly and harshly she sang, but it was sweet music to the king, for it told him the name of his enemy. He crept past the cave, and then he ran down the whole way to the city. It was dark by then, and the goblin was up on the spire, fixing the gilded weathercock that was to finish the building. The king stood, and called at the top of his voice: "Set it straight, *Foul-Weather*." At that the goblin fell straight from the high tower and was shattered into a thousand smithereens as if he had been made of glass. And the golden weathercock on the high steeple is crooked to this day.

G

Gabriel Hounds. In the late Autumn great flocks of wild geese and other birds fly down the wide rivers on their way south, and in the early Spring they come up again to their nesting places in the north, and the quick beat of their wings and the cries they make to each other to keep together sound like the yelping and barking of hounds high up in the air. In old days people used to believe that these noises were made by ghostly hounds with human heads who flew high up in the air, hunting the souls of unrepentant sinners. If they hovered over a house it was thought to be a death token, and people who were out alone at night and heard them pass

overhead were terrified. They were called different names in different parts of the country: the Gabriel Hounds, the Gabriel Ratchets, the DEVIL'S DANDY DOGS, the Sky-Yelpers and, in Wales, Cwn Annwn, the dogs of Hell. Whatever they were called, people were glad to seek the shelter of a house when they crossed over, but most people now know that they are only birds and wish them good fortune on their perilous journey.

Giants. Giants are of a great many kinds and characters, but they have one thing in common, they are all enormously large and strong, though some of course are much larger than others. Bran the Blessed of Wales was enormous, but both good and wise. When he waded across the straits to Ireland to punish the Irish for the way in which they had ill-used his sister, Branwen, the Irish swineherds took him for a mountain moving towards the shore with a forest waving above it and two lakes divided by a sharp ridge, but Branwen could explain that the lakes were his eyes, opened wide in anger, and the sharp ridge was his nose. He was so large that no boat could carry him and no house could hold him, but he was sweet and gentle by nature and one of the best kings that ever ruled Britain. When he had died from a poisoned dart his followers carried his head back to London to bury it under the White Tower, and as long as it was there no invasion could trouble Britain, and all the time that his followers carried it they were as happy as if Bran himself was with them.

Bran was the best and wisest of all the giants, but there were others who were kindly, if rather simple, and who protected their little mortal neighbours from evil giants and even from the Devil himself. One of the most famous of these was the Giant of Grabbist, who carried the stones for Hawkridge Church and had great stone-throwing competitions with the Devil. The Devil cheated when he could, but the giant was too sharp for him and he won in the end and then he picked Old Nick up by the tail, swung him three times round his head and sent him flying off almost to the Barbadoes. "He's back now," they say, "but he's a bit shy of poking his nose into Somerset, for fear the old giant should still be there."

There are other stories of kindly giants, who seem to have got more simple-minded as time went on. There is a story in Cornwall of the old giant of Carn Galva who set up a logan-stone – one that rocks to and fro – to use as a rocking chair, and had a great pile of square stones which he used as building bricks, piling them up and kicking them down again to amuse himself, for he had no wife and used to get lonesome. There was a boy living near who knew the giant was a kind old fellow and used to come over and visit him sometimes to play at bob with quoits, or at hide-and-seek, which the giant called "mop-and-heed". But the giant did not know his strength. One day they had had a great game, and at last the boy threw down his quoit and said he must go home. The giant in great good humour tapped him on the head and said, "Be sure to come tomorrow, my son, and us will have a capital game of bob." But as he said the word "bob" his playmate fell to the ground dead, for the giant's fingers had crushed his skull right in. The old giant went down on his knees and tried to mend his head with clay, but it was no use, and he picked up the boy and sat down on the logan-stone rocking him up and down and crying and sobbing out, "Oh, my son, my son, why didn't they make the shell of thy noddle stronger? A' is as soft as a pie-crust, dough-baked, and made too thin by half! However shall I pass the time without thee to play bob and mop-and-heed?" After that the poor old giant took no interest in anything, and before the year was over he had pined away and died.

These kind giants were not as common as the fierce, man-eating ogres, some of them two-headed or three-headed monsters, who ground men's bones for bread and were the terror of the countryside. These were the kind that Jack the Giant Killer fought with and from whom Jack of the Beanstalk stole his treasures. Some of

these kept human beings as servants, but they were chiefly interested in them as food. Most of these giants were stupid and easily tricked, but a few, rather smaller in size, were magicians and could only be defeated by other magic. Often the heroes who defeated these giant–magicians were helped by animals to whom they had been kind, for in fairy stories kindness nearly always brings its reward, and fairy stories, fantastic as they are, often tell us a good deal about real life.

Goblins. Goblins are evil and malicious spirits who delight in frightening and hurting people. They are generally small but very strong, and they are almost always ugly. They live underground in caves and mines. The goblins in George Macdonald's book *The Princess and the Goblin* are very true to the country people's belief about them, and so are those in *The Hobbit*. If "hob" is put in front of the name the sting is taken out of it, for HOBS are friendly spirits. The Puritans thought all fairies were wicked, so John Bunyan tells of "Hobgoblins or foul fiends", but they were mistaken about this. Hobgoblins can be rather mischievous and fond of practical jokes, but they are merry, good-natured little creatures as a rule; and they do not live underground in caves, but like to play about in human houses and help people who deserve to be helped.

Green Children. Two of the early chroniclers tell a strange story about some fairy children who were found near Wolf-pits in Suffolk at the beginning of the twelfth century. They were a boy and a girl like ordinary people in size and shape except that they were light green all over. Some country people found them lying dazed and frightened at the mouth of a cave. They talked in a strange language and did not seem to understand anything that was said to them, so the people took them to a knight, Sir Richard de Calne, who had a castle at Wikes. They seemed very hungry, but they would not touch bread or meat, only cried bitterly. At last by chance some broad beans were brought into the house, and they seemed eager for those, and when people opened the pods and showed them the beans inside they ate them hungrily. The boy was sad and weak, and soon pined away, but the girl learned to eat human food and to speak the Anglo-Norman language, and in time she lost her green colour and looked like everyone else. She was christened, and when she grew old enough she was married and settled down. People asked her how she had come there, and she told them something about her country.

She said that the land they lived in was called St Martin's Land, and the people there were Christians. There was no sun or moon but a kind of twilight like that before sunrise. All the country and the creatures in it were green, and the people were pale green too. One day they were watching their flocks when they came to the mouth of a cavern, and a sweet sound came out, the chiming of distant bells, which they had never heard before, and they followed it on and on till suddenly they turned a corner and came into the full light of the sun. The dazzling light and the rush of moving air dazed and stunned them and they fell down on the ground. Then they heard loud voices and they tried to run away, but they could not see their way in the dazzling light, and they turned to and fro until the people caught them. At first they were very frightened, but the girl soon understood that they meant to be kind, and in the end she settled down into their strange ways.

Habetrot. Habetrot was the patron fairy of spinners in the Border Country. She was not like Tom Tit Tot or Whuppity Stoorie, who drove a hard bargain with people they helped, but was ready to do people a good turn and was not even hard upon girls who did not like spinning themselves.

There was once a merry, idle lassie in Selkirkshire who liked roaming over the country gathering flowers much better than blistering her fingers with spinning. The goodwife, her mother, was a great spinster, but lessons did nothing, and at last she lost her temper and drove the lassie up to her bedroom, carried up a

spinning wheel and seven heads of lint and said to the lassie, "Noo ma lass ye'll spin me seven skeins oot o' yon lint in three days or 'twill be the worse for you." And she left her there, crying her eyes out.

The lassie knew well that her minnie was in earnest, so for a long day she worked away at the wheel, but she only got sore fingers from twisting the thread and sore lips pulling it out and about three feet of lumpy, uneven thread that no one in her senses would try to knit or weave. So the poor lassie cried herself to sleep. In the morning she woke up very early, and the sun was shining and the birds were singing, and she looked at the poor bit of thread she had spun and she thought to herself: "I can do no good here; I'll out into the cool air." So she crept down the ladder and past the curtains of her mother's box-bed, unbolted the kitchen door, and ran down to the burnside. She wandered here and there, plucking the wild primroses and listening to the birds singing, until she suddenly thought that however long she loitered she would have to go back home at last, and how angry her mother would be. There was a little mound in front of her and she sat down on a smooth, self-bored stone by the burnside and burst into tears. A self-bored stone is one where the water has made a deep, narrow hole in the rock. People used to say that you can see fairies through a self-bored stone. However that may be the lassie began to hear sounds coming from it, and a kind of whirring, and shrill little voices singing a strange tune. She looked up and there was a strange little woman working busily at her spindle and pulling out the thread with a long lip that looked as if it was made for spinning. "A fair gude day to ye, gudewife," said the lassie, who was always friendly and well-spoken. "And to you too, my dawtie," said the little woman, well pleased with her. "What for are ye sae lang-lippit?" said the lassie, like the bairn that she was. "Wi' pulling oot the thread, my hinnie," said the old wifie. "That's what I sud be doing," said the lassie, "but it's nae gude, I can mak' naething of it." And she told the whole story.

"Never heed, my hinnie," said the kind old wife. "Fetch me yir lint, and I'll hae it a' spun up in good time for yir mither." So the lassie ran up and slipped into the cottage, and back with the lint in a flash. "What will I call ye, gude-wife?" she said. "And whaur will I come for the skeins?" But the old wife took the lint and was gone. The lassie was quite dazed and she sat down on the stone to wait. The sun was hot on her head, and after a while she fell fast asleep and never stirred till the sun went down in the sky and the air began to grow chill. She waked to hear the whirring and singing louder than before, and a ray of light was coming out of the self-bored stone. So she knelt up and put an eye to it and saw a strange sight through the peephole. She was looking down into a great cavern, and a number of queer figures were sitting at their spinning wheels, spin-spinning away like mad. They all had long, long lips and flat thumbs and hunched backs, and her friend was walking about among them. There was one that was sitting a little apart from the rest and uglier than anyone, and her name was Scantlie Mab, for that's what the head fairy called her. "They're nearly finished, Scantlie Mab," she said and then she laughed and cried out, "Little kens the wee lassie on the brae-head that Habetrot is my name! Bundle up the yarn and give it to me, for I must take it up to the wee lassie at her minnie's door."

Then the lassie knew where they were to meet, and she ran up to her cottage, and she'd hardly been there a moment before Habetrot appeared and gave her seven beautiful hanks of yarn. "Oh what can I do for you in return?" said the lassie. "Dinna tell yir Mither wha spun the skeins," said Habetrot, "and cry on me whiles if ye need me." And she was gone into the darkness.

Her mother had gone to bed early, for she had been working hard all day making black puddings – "black sausters" they called them in that part of the world – and seven beautiful black puddings were hanging up to dry from the rafters. The girl was as hungry as a hunter, for she had had nothing since breakfast the day before. She spread out the beautiful skeins where her Mother would see them first thing when she woke, then she blew up the fire and took down the frying-pan and cooked the first sauster and ate it, and she was hungrier than ever. Then she cooked the next, and the next, and suddenly she discovered that she had eaten them all. So she tiptoed up the ladder to bed and fell asleep as soon as her head had touched the pillow.

The mother woke up next morning, and when she drew back the curtains of her bed she saw the seven beautiful skeins, better than any spinster in the country could spin them, and she cast up her eyes in amazement – and where were the fine black puddings that were hanging up there last night? Not one was to be seen, only a black frying-pan standing at the side of the fire.

She ran out into the road in her bed-gown like one demented, and cried out:

> "Ma dawtie ha' spun se'en, se'en, se'en!
> Ma dawtie ha' ate se'en, se'en, se'en,
> An a' afore daylicht."

She sang out so loud that it woke her daughter, who got up and began to dress as quick as she could.

And who should come riding along the road but the young laird himself. "What's that you're crying, goodwife?" he said; and she sang out again:

> "Ma dawtie's spun se'en, se'en, se'en,
> Ma dawtie's eaten se'en, se'en!"

An' if ye don't believe me, laird, come and see for yersel!"

So the laird followed her into the cottage and when he saw the beautiful skeins he asked to see the spinner, and when he saw the spinner he asked her to marry him.

The laird was braw and brave and kind, and the lass was glad to say yes; but there was one thing that troubled her, the laird kept talking of all the fine yarn she would be spinning after the wedding. So one day the lassie went down to the self-bored stone and called for Habetrot. Habetrot knew what her trouble would be, but she said, "Never need, hinnie; bring your jo here and we'll sort it for ye."

So next night at sunset the pair of them stood at the self-bored stone, and heard Habetrot singing, and at the end of the song she opened a hidden door and let them into the mound. The laird was astonished at all the hideous shapes around him, and said to the lassie, "Why are their lips all deformed?" Habetrot said aloud,

"Ask them yourself." And each one said in muttering or whistling tones, ".Wi' spin-spin-spinning."

"Aye, aye, they were once bonnie enough," said Habetrot, "but spinners aye gang that gait. Yir ain lassie'll be the same, bonnie as she is noo, for she's fair mad aboot the spinning."

"She'll not!" said the laird. "Not another spindle shall she touch from this day on."

"Just as ye say, laird," said the lassie, and from that day she roamed the countryside with the laird, and rode about behind him as blithe as a bird, and every head of lint that grew on that land went to old Habetrot to be spun.

Hedley Kow. The Hedley Kow was a real bogey-beast, a Yorkshire one, who haunted the village of Hedley near Ebchester. He was not a dangerous bogie, but he was very mischievous and full of fun, and he played more practical jokes than you could think of in a long summer's day. Certainly he was rather a nuisance on a farm. He would take the shape of a favourite cow and lead the milkmaid a terrible dance round the field, then he would kick over the pail, slip the rope that was holding him and frolic away over the field on four great long legs, whickering like a pony and laughing like a ROBIN GOODFELLOW. He would overturn the milk pails, give the cream to the cats and sit in the churn so that the butter would not come. People used to be furious at his tricks, and a little bit frightened too, but there was one person who got the better of him, for whatever tricks he played he could not frighten her or make her angry.

There was a poor little old woman near Hedley who was often hungry and often cold and made her living by running errands and doing odd jobs for the neighbours, but she was always happy and cheerful and as brisk as a bird. One afternoon she was trotting along after taking round some shopping she'd done for the neighbours when she passed a great big iron pot lying in the ditch. "Well," she said, "who's left a good pot like this lying here?" Even if it had a hole in it it'd do to plant a flower in. She looked around to see if there was anyone near who could own it, and as there was no one she thought she'd try to get it home, but when she tried to lift it it was too heavy. She took the lid off, and the pot was chock-full of gold pieces. "Well I never!" said she. "Such a piece of luck would only happen to me! But there, I was born lucky. If I can only get it home I'll be as rich as the Queen for the rest of my days." The pot was too heavy to lift, so she tied her shawl to the handle and began to drag it along the road, thinking of all the great things she would do with the money.

After a time she had to stop for lack of breath, and she bent down to look at her treasure. She could hardly believe her eyes. The iron pot and the lid and the gold had all gone, and in their place was a great bar of shining silver. "Silver!" she said. "Well on my word that's safer than gold. The neighbours would all stare if I'd come out with gold pieces to spend. Robbers would have come round the place in no time. No, no, I can carry the bar of silver up to town, and get shillings and sixpences that will keep me from want for many a day. Yes, yes, it's a lucky change however it happened." She tightened her shawl round the silver and trotted on.

By and by it began to follow her less smoothly, and she looked round again. It wasn't a smooth bar of silver, but a great jagged piece of rusty iron. She bent down and touched it. "Well!" she said. "That's strange, my eyes must be playing me tricks. I'd have sworn it was bright, shining silver, and it's nothing but a piece of rusty iron. And much better and safer it is too!" She said, "I'd maybe have been puzzled to find someone to buy the silver, but I know just who'll give me good pennies, and plenty of 'em, for a great piece of old iron like this. Yes, I'm in luck no doubt, and it's lucky I've been all my life," and on she trotted.

As she turned the corner into her own lane she looked round, and there was a great smooth stone wrapped up in the end of her shawl. "Lawk a mercy!" she said. "What is it but a stone after all! Why it's just the very shape and size of stone I've been wanting this while back to prop open my garden gate that keeps slamming on me. Well, on my word, I am lucky!" And she trotted on, pushed open the garden gate, pulled the stone inside and bent down to undo her shawl. There lay the stone, as still and quiet as a stone could be. Then suddenly it gave a kind of whicker and a shiver; four long lanky legs shot up under it, a long wispy tail shot out at one end and a head shot out at the other and two long ears shot out of the head, and off frisked the Hedley Kow, whickering and neighing and laughing like a naughty schoolboy. The old woman stared after it, and then she burst out into a loud laugh too. "Well! To think of me seeing the Hedley Kow after all these years, and making so bold with it too. Well, I've been in luck today and no mistake! I do feel that grand! That uplifted!" And she marched into her cottage as proud as a queen.

Henkies. Henkies was a nickname given to the Shetland TROWS. They were grotesque little people who limped, or "henked", as they walked. Their dance music was very catchy but their dances were very queer, for they clasped their hands round their knees and did a kind of goose-dance, bobbing wildly up and down. There is a story about a little trow who peeped wistfully at a mortal dance until she could bear it no longer and bounded into the room, bobbing up and down and setting at one man after another. But she looked so strange and wild, twisting and turning and bouncing there, that they all drew back and left a space in the middle of the room, where she bobbed and bounced, singing out at the top of her voice:

> " 'Hey!' co Cuttie; an' 'ho!' co Cuttie;
> 'An' wha 'ill dance wi' me?' co Cuttie.
> She luked aboot an' saw naebody;
> 'Sae I'll henk awa mesel',' co Cuttie."

So poor little Cuttie knew her nickname all right.

Hobs or Hobgoblins. The whole tribe of friendly, domesticated spirits, who do work for men, though they are often rather fond of practical jokes, are hobs. Some people call them "hobmen" and some "hobgoblins". BROWNIES are hobs, and most of the hobmen behave in much the same way as brownies, though they all have their own individual habits. There was one, for instance, who lived in a hobhole at Runswick Bay near Hartlepool and was a specialist in whooping cough. The parents of a child who was very ill with this could bring it into the cave and whisper into the hobhole:

> "Hob-hole Hob! Hob-hole Hob!
> Ma bairn's gotten t'kink cough,
> Tak't off; tak't off!"

After that the child would get better very quickly.

Many of the hobs behave just like brownies. There was one, for instance, who lived at Sturfit Hall, near Reeth in Yorkshire. He

churned the milk, made up the fires and did all the other brownie jobs. He was stark naked, and the mistress of the Hall was sorry for him and left out a cloak and hood for him. He put them on, and they heard him saying:

> "Ha! a cloak and a hood,
> Hob'll never do mair good."

And he never came back to work.

Another of them, near Danby, didn't like the quality of the clothes put out for him, for his rhyme went:

> Gin Hob mun hae nowt but harding hamp,
> He'll come nae mair to berry nor stamp.

There was also a hobthrust, who lived in a cave called Hobthrust Hall and worked for the landlord of an inn half a mile away. His wages were a large slice of bread and butter. One night they forgot to leave it for him and he never came to work again.

Hobgoblins really belong to the hobmen, though the Puritans thought that hobgoblins were devils; but they did not really approve of any fairies. Hobgoblins are more fond of practical jokes than brownies and are rather ready to turn into BOGGARTS if they are teased or annoyed. Boggarts might just be allowed to be called hobmen, but BOGIES and BOGLES have slipped over the edge and belong to the UNSEELIE COURT.

Imps or Impets. In old days an "imp" meant a cutting or an off-shoot. An "ympe" tree was an apple tree that was grown from a cutting or grafted on to a growing tree already rooted, and there was thought to be something magical about it. An imp meant a

little devil, an off-shoot of Satan. Tom Tit Tot is called an impet, and he was a little black thing, full of malice. GOBLINS and BOGIES are sometimes called imps, but they are little, young devils according to the old story-teller.

King Herla. The story of King Herla is one of the earliest stories told about a visit to Fairyland and the strange swiftness with which time passed in that enchanted realm.

King Herla was a famous and powerful king of the Ancient Britons. One day, as he was out hunting, a strange figure rode up to him on a goat. He was less than half the size of a man, with hairy legs ending in goats' hoofs, a big head and a long bushy red beard, and he was wearing a spotted fawn-skin. He was no beauty, but he spoke very politely and behaved like a king.

"Hail, King Herla! I am the lord of mighty realms and numberless people, and I am glad to carry a message of love and friendship to you from them all, for your own virtues have raised you above all kings, and you are the best of all who rule in this upper world. To do you honour I mean to be guest at your wedding next year. You do not yet know that you are to be married so soon, but we know it. The ambassadors of the King of France are already on their way to offer you the hand of his beautiful daughter. They will arrive tomorrow, and I will attend your wedding, and exactly a year from then you will attend mine. Farewell for a year." With that he turned as swiftly as a tiger and disappeared.

The next day, as he had said, the embassy of the King of France arrived and offered King Herla the hand of his daughter, who was the wonder of the Western World for beauty and goodness. So the marriage was arranged, and in just under a year the bride had arrived and the pair were wedded with great joy and merriment. As they sat at the table before the wedding feast began, suddenly the Pigmy King was there with a great crowd of his followers, so many that they filled every seat at the High Table and crowded the Great Hall, and as many again were out in the courtyard, in silk tents which they had set up in a twinkling. Gaily dressed servants darted out of these tents with rich wine and better food than any man there had ever tasted. The Princess of France and the guests at the banquet had never been so served in their lives. The pigmies were everywhere where they were wanted and nowhere where they were not wanted. They brought musicians who played the sweetest music, and rich gifts which they heaped before the bride. Everyone praised them and said they had never known anything to match it. And nothing was taken from King Herla's store, all was brought by the pigmies. At length, when everyone had eaten as much as he could eat, the Pigmy said to King Herla, "Most excellent King, I have fulfilled my promise. If there is anything else that you desire, you have only to wish and it is yours. I only ask that a year from today you shall be ready to honour my wedding as I have honoured yours." When he had said this they all went swiftly to their tents, and the next day before cockcrow they had gone.

King Herla did not forget his promise. All that year he gathered together presents worthy to give to such a noble friend, and on the very day the Pigmy King appeared with a troop of followers, and Herla and his knights set out with him, laden with gifts. They had not gone very far before they reached a high cliff, and suddenly an opening appeared and they all rode into a high, dark cave lit by torches. They rode on until they came out of the cave into a green meadow, and a great castle stood in front of them. The Fairy King greeted King Herla with kind words and led him into a splendid palace. There the wedding was held and they feasted and made merry for three whole days and nights. King Herla gave his gifts and the Fairy King gave him gifts in return, and at length, loaded with treasures, they were led along the dark cave again. Before he left them, their guide gave King Herla a little hound, small enough to sit before him on the saddle, and said, "The King, my master, sends this message, that you are none of you to dismount from your horses until this hound leaps from the saddle."

With that he left them, and they rode through the opening, which closed behind them.

They rode on until they saw a peasant working, and King Herla summoned him and asked what news there was of his queen, naming her by name. The peasant stood for a moment, then said: "Sir, I hardly understand you, for you speak in the old Welsh tongue and I myself am a Saxon, one of those who conquered this land two hundred years ago. As for the queen you speak of, I only heard of but one of that name, and she married a king called Herla who ruled the land long ago. Men say he went into a cave in that high cliff many long years ago, and never was heard of since."

When they heard that, some of Herla's knights leapt to the ground, and as their feet touched it the weight of their years came on them, and they crumbled into dust. Then Herla called to his knights not to dismount, and rode on. Men sometimes see them riding madly through the land, waiting for the little hound to leap down; but it has never left the saddle, and they say it will never leave it until the Day of Judgement.

Knockers. There were supposed to be a great number of little spirits who worked in the Cornish tin mines, blasting, picking, shovelling, wheeling away tin-ore for themselves. They worked day and night, as busy as bees, but the miners thought it was lucky to have them about the place, for where their knocking was heard there was sure to be rich ore found. They were given all sorts of names: bockles, buccas, gathorns, knockers, nickers, nuggies and spriggans. As a rule they were only heard, but every now and then someone saw them and even managed to talk to them. There was one end of the mine near Bosprenis where some bockles were particularly busy, and people thought that there must be a very rich lode there, but most people were afraid to venture because it was known that the knockers, like most fairy people, did not like to be spied on. But there were two men, a father and son called Trenwith, who ventured to the lode at midnight one Midsummer Eve and watched till they saw "the smae people" bringing up the shining ore. Old Trenwith had a way with the fairies, and he spoke

to them civilly and told them that he could save them all the trouble of breaking down the ore if they would allow him and his boy to work that lode. He would quarry out the ore, clean it and leave a tenth of all he got wherever they wanted to have it. They agreed, and he treated them fairly, and he and his son soon grew rich on their share of the ore.

All went well as long as the old man was alive, but after he died the son began to grudge their fair share to the knockers, and they did not take long to find out that they were being cheated. Then the lode dried up and the son could find no tin anywhere in his part of the mine. He took to drink, and in the end he died a beggar. It is as well to deal fairly with the Little People.

Lady of the Lake. The Lady of the Lake is one of the most mysterious and unexplained of the fairy ladies who flit in and out of the stories of King Arthur and his knights. In the earlier legends these were real fairies, but as time went on they were more and more treated as mortal enchantresses. Malory says of Morgan le Fai, for instance, that when she was a girl she went to school in a convent and was taught magic; but originally Le Fata Morgana was a fairy, almost a goddess, who raised storms at sea. In the earliest romance of Sir Lancelot, the Lady of the Lake was a water fairy who stole the baby Lancelot from his fainting mother and carried him away to a magic island in the middle of the lake – an Isle of Maidens like that in the Irish legends – where she brought him up so that he should conquer the enemy who was harassing her cowardly son. In a later story she is said to be an enchantress who raises the appearance of a lake about her by glamour. She is a tricky, puzzling character, because she seems generally to be an enemy of Arthur, but it was she who gave him his sword Excalibur, and she was one of the three queens who appeared, summoned by his sword, to carry him away in a barge to the Isle of Avalon to be healed of his wounds.

Lambton Worm. In Scotland and the North of England dragons were called "worms", because the Saxon and Norse name for a dragon was *worm*. Sometimes these worms had wings, but generally they were like enormous, elongated lizards, so long that they could coil themselves several times round a small hill. There are a good many stories of these worms – some even come from Somerset – but the story of the Lambton Worm is the best because it begins at the very beginning and ends at the end, even after the death of the Worm.

In the fourteenth century the Heir of Lambton in Weardale was a wild lad who delighted in doing things that would shock people, and one fine Sunday he was sitting fishing in the river Wear just outside the castle walls, in full sight of all the tenants who were crossing the bridge over the river on their way to church. He had fished and fished and caught nothing all morning, and just as the bells were stopping he burst into a stream of terrible oaths, so that the last churchgoers hurried into church so as not to hear him. As the bell gave the last peal he hooked something on his line, and he landed it after a terrible struggle. It was not a fish, but such a hideous thing that he broke his line and threw it into the well near by. Just then a stranger passed by and stopped to ask what luck he had had. "I think I've caught the devil," said the Heir. "Just look into that well there." The stranger peered down at the thing threshing about in the water. "It looks like a great eft [a newt]," said the stranger, "except that it's got nine holes round its mouth. If you ask me I'd say that it bodes no good." And he went on his way.

Time passed. The Heir of Lambton seemed a sobered man after that day, and before long he went to the Holy Land. In the well the eft grew and grew until it was too big to stay there, and it came out and curled itself round Worm's Hill, from which it ravaged the countryside. They put a great trough outside the castle gate, and filled it each day with the milk of nine cows, but that did not satisfy the Worm. Brave knights came to destroy it, but when it was cut in two it joined together again, as worms do, and it crushed them to death.

At length the Heir returned, a Knight of Rhodes now, and he was horrified to hear of all the evil he had done by his folly. He was determined to destroy the Worm, but when he heard how all the brave knights that went against it had been slaughtered he went to a wise woman who lived near and asked her to tell him how best to go about it. He had to endure a fierce scolding from

her first, but in the end she softened and told him just what he must do. First he must go to the chapel and take a solemn vow to kill the first living creature that he met on his return from the combat. If he failed to do this no Lord of Lambton would die in his bed for nine generations. Then he must go to a smith and have his armour covered all over with spikes of iron. When that was done he must take his stand on the great rock that stood in the middle of the river Wear, and from there he must attack the Worm when he came down to drink in his usual pool at sunset.

The Heir did as the wise woman said, and to be sure that a worthy sacrifice should be ready he told the servants that when he came back successful he would blow his horn when he reached the castle and they must loose his favourite hound to meet him. Then he went down and climbed on to the rock. The great monster dragged his long coils down to the river and bent his snaky head to drink. The Heir brought his sword down on the back of his head, and at the first touch the Worm shot forward and wrapped himself round his enemy. As he tightened his folds he gashed himself on the spikes, and the more he squeezed the more his blood gushed out, till the river Wear ran red. Bit by bit the Heir hacked him in pieces and the strong current bore them away so that they could not join.

At length the battle was over, and the Heir staggered home, so exhausted that he had hardly strength to blow his horn. But his old father, who had been waiting in terrible suspense, heard the faint blast and ran out to embrace his son. The Heir blew a second blast, the servants heard it and loosed the dog, who came bounding out and died on his master's sword. But the old father had greeted him first, the oath was broken, and for nine generations no Lord of Lambton died in his bed.

Lepracaun. The lepracaun and the CLURICAUNE are two little solitary Irish fairies, but the cluricaune likes to lurk in cellars, like a BUTTERY SPIRIT, while the lepracaun is the fairy shoemaker, who is supposed to have won great wealth for himself. If he can be caught and held he will yield it up, but the difficulty is that if you look away from him for a moment while you are carrying him

to the spot where his treasure is hidden, he will slip out of your
hand like a drop of water and you will not find him again. William
Allingham, who wrote the poem beginning

> Up the airy mountain,
> Down the rushy glen,
> We daren't go a hunting
> For fear of Little Men,

also wrote a very good poem about the lepracaun which gives one
a notion of many stories that have been told about him and a
splendid description of the little fellow himself:

> I caught him at work one day, myself,
>   In the castle-ditch, where foxglove grows, –
> A wrinkled, wizen'd, and bearded Elf,
>   Spectacles stuck on his pointed nose,
>   Silver buckles to his hose,
>   Leather apron – shoe in his lap –
>   "Rip-rap, tip-tap,
>   Tack-tack-too!
>   (A grasshopper on my cap!
>   Away the moth flew!)
>   Buskins for a fairy prince,

    Brogues for his son, –
  Pay me well, pay me well,
    When the job is done!"
The rogue was mine, beyond a doubt,
I stared at him; he stared at me;
"Servant, Sir!" "Humph!" says he,
  And pull'd a snuff-box out.
He took a long pinch, look'd better pleased,
  The queer little Lepracaun;
Offer'd the box with a whimsical grace, –
Pouf! he flung the dust in my face,
    And, while I sneezed,
      Was gone!

And in some such way most meetings with the lepracaun end.

Mermaids. Everyone knows what a mermaid looks like, but there are different ideas about her behaviour and character. From the waist up she is a beautiful maiden with long golden hair, but below the waist she has the body and tail of a fish. She often carries a comb in one hand and a glass in the other, and will sit on a rock in the sea, combing her hair, looking at herself in the mirror and singing in a voice of such enchanting sweetness that men can hardly help plunging into the sea and swimming out to her. The sight of her is often a sign of storms, as many people will know by the folk-song called "The Mermaid":

> One Friday morn our ship set sail,
> And our boat not far from the land,
> We there did espy a fair pretty maid,
>   With a comb and a glass in her hand, her hand, her hand,
>   With a comb and a glass in her hand.

At the sight of her the whole crew despaired, from the captain down to the little cabin-boy, and they were right, for the ship spun round and "sank to the bottom of the sea".

This was one of the hungry, ravening mermaids. Some of these haunt fresh water as well as salt, and swim up streams and into fresh-water lakes, and you will sometimes see a mermaid lying on the banks of a river miles from the sea. They are still called "mermaids", so probably their natural home is the sea, but they can be as dangerous in fresh water as in salt, as the Laird of Lorntie nearly learnt to his cost.

The young Laird of Lorntie, in Forfarshire, was riding back one evening, with his serving-man behind him, from a hunting expedition when he passed a little lake, or "lochan", which lies about three miles south of Lorntie in the middle of a wood. As he rode along the track passing it he heard screams coming from the wood and turned his horse's head towards the lake, where he saw a beautiful woman struggling in the water. She seemed to know the Laird, for she screamed, "Help, Lorntie! Help Lorntie! Help Lorn–" and here the water seemed to choke her as she disappeared.

The Laird leapt off his horse and flung himself into the lochan, and was just grasping the beautiful golden locks that were floating on the water when he was seized from behind by his servant and forced out of the loch. He was furious, but his man called out, "Bide a wee, Lorntie! Bide a wee! That wauling madam was no other, God save us! than the mermaid." Lorntie looked back at the gold-bright locks floating on the water and could see at once that they grew on no human head. "You're in the right," he said, and climbed back on his horse. As they turned their heads away from the lochan, the mermaid rose up out of the water and cried in a fiendish voice:

"Lorntie, Lorntie,
　Were it na your man,
I had gart your heart's blood
　Skirl in my pan."

That was a blood-drinking mermaid, but not all of them were as wicked. Some of them are kind to young lovers, and know a great deal about herbs. There is a story about a beautiful young girl in Galloway who was very ill, and her lover was sitting by the river mourning for her when a kind mermaid rose up in the water and sang very sweetly:

"Would ye let the bonnie may die in your hand
And the mugwort flowering in the land?"

He understood her and went at once to a garden where the mugwort was in flower, pressed and steeped it, and gave the liquid to the girl to drink. In a short while she recovered, and southernwood has been known ever since as a cure for diseases of the lungs. Another gentle mermaid who had a great knowledge of herbs is mentioned in the Cornish story of the OLD MAN OF CURY, in which the mermaid was grateful and kind, but the merman was a much more ferocious character.

Merrows. The merpeople of Ireland were called merrows. The female merrows are beautiful as the MERMAIDS are, though they have fishes' tails and little webs between their fingers. They are dreaded as mermaids are, because they generally appear before storms, but they are gentler than many of the mermaids, and they sometimes fall in love with mortals and marry them. They can come to land as pretty little cattle, but when they come in their own proper shape they wear caps made of red feathers so that

they can come through the sea from their dry underwater country. If their feather caps are stolen when they are on the land they cannot go back to their homes any more than the SELKIES can when their sealskins are hidden. It used to be said that the descendants of the merrow wives could be told by their scaly legs and their web-fingers.

If the female merrows are beautiful, the male ones are very ugly indeed. They have green faces and bodies, red sharp noses and eyes like a pig. They are very jovial, merry fellows, however, and there were human beings who became very fond of their merrow friends. Crofton Croker, who collected and told a great many lively stories at about the same time when Jacob and William Grimm were making their great collection of German fairy tales, tells a good story about the friendship between a man and a merrow which is called "Soul Cages". It is very lively but rather long, so that I have to shorten it a little, but it is worth reading in full.

There was once a man who was very anxious to see a merrow and make friends with him, and that was Jack Dogherty, who lived with his wife Biddy in a snug little cabin close to the sea near Ennis. The thing was that his own grandfather had been great friends with a merrow, and had been so chief with him that he would have asked the old fellow to stand godfather to his son if it hadn't been for offending the priest, and yet poor Jack, who lived in the very same place, could never get so much as a glimpse of him, for all his looking and listening. Still, Jack did not lose heart and he kept hanging about the place looking with all his eyes until one day, about half a mile along the coast, he seemed to see a figure standing on a rock well out to sea that looked to have a red cocked hat on its head. He could not be altogether certain, for the thing stood so still that it might be a queer-shaped rock and the red hat might be the dazzle of the sunset in his eyes. Then the sun in his eyes made him sneeze, and the thing shot off the rock in a flash, and he knew it was the merrow indeed. After that he spent every spare minute by that rock, and he found a way of getting nearer to it, and sometimes he would watch it for quite a while, but it seemed he would never get speech with it. Then at last one day the merrow spoke directly to him as friendly as a Christian: "Good day to you, Jack Dogherty, and how have you been keeping this while?"

"Sure, your Honour's very pat with my name," said Jack, surprised.

"And why wouldn't I be pat with it, when your grandfather and myself was like two brothers together," said the merrow. "That was a grand man, Jack, he could drink any man round Ennis under the table. I wonder do you take after him, Jack?"

"I'll not say I'm altogether his equal," said Jack, "but if it's a matter of liking good drink and plenty of it, I think I'm pretty near him. But where is it you get your drink under the sea, your Honour? I'm thinking there's little there but salt water, and that's not to everyone's taste."

"Where is it you get your own, Jack?" said the old chap with a wink.

Now Jack got the greater part of what he drank – and sold too – out of casks that rolled up to his cabin door. He wasn't one to rob or hurt poor sailors, but he had no objection to taking what they had no further use for. So he winked back at the old fellow, and said, "Oh, I take your meaning, your Honour, but I'm thinking you'll need a long cellar to take all the sea gives you."

"So I do, Jack, and if you like to come here this time next Monday you shall have a look at my cellar, and a taste of what's in it into the bargain." With that he waved his scaly hand and dived down into the sea.

There is no doubt that Jack was there before the time next Monday, but the merrow was there before him, with two cocked hats under his arm.

"Here you are, Jack," he said, "I've borrowed a second hat for you, so we can come down together."

Jack held back for a minute, frightened to take the plunge. The old merrow said scornfully, "You're not a quarter the man your grandfather was before you!" So Jack plucked up his courage, jammed the hat on his head, laid hold on the merrow's tail and down they went, down and down through the water till they were on a dry, sandy plain with great weeds growing out of it like trees, and the fishes swimming about over their heads. The merrow's neat little house was in front of them with smoke curling up the chimney, so they went inside and found a grand dinner of all kinds of fish waiting for them, and drink of all kinds too. Jack Dogherty had never felt himself cooler, but the old merrow got very merry and yelled out all kinds of songs. He told Jack his name too, which was Coomara – Coo to his friends, for by this time they were pretty snug together.

After they'd drunken as much as they wanted, Coomara took Jack round his house to look at all his curiosities, and a pretty collection he had of all sorts of things that had dropped down out of the sea, but the thing that puzzled Jack most was rows of curious wicker cages that looked rather like lobster pots.

"What do you keep in those?" Jack asked.

"Oh, those are soul cages," said Coomara.

"What are soul cages?" said Jack, who'd never heard of such a thing. "Fish don't have souls."

"No, of course they haven't," said Coomara, "but men have. Those are the souls of fishermen. When there's a storm up above I sprinkle these about, and if they lose their way and come down here they feel all lost and lorn and they creep in there and it fails them to get out again, and aren't they lucky now to be here all warm and dry when they might be plunging about in the cold, wet sea?"

Jack never said a word, but he stooped down to look into the cages and there was nothing he could see, but when Coomara said that the souls were lucky to be there he heard a kind of sob coming from the cage nearest to him, and it grieved him to the heart to think of all those poor souls imprisoned there when they should have been on their way to Heaven. So he said good night to Coomara, who gave him a push up into the sea, and he shot home as quick as a flash.

All next day Jack thought and pondered how he could get those poor souls free. And at last it came to him that he must invite Coomara to his house and drink him under the table, and whilst he was asleep he'd take the cap off his head and slip down under the sea and let out the imprisoned souls. So he told Biddy his wife that he'd been thinking about all the poor sailors that had been drowned and that he would like her to go a pilgrimage to pray for them. Biddy was very pleased to do that, and the day after she'd gone he put out all the drink he had and went down to Coomara's rock and invited him to come and taste his liquor. Coomara was very ready to come, and though Jack wasn't lucky the first day, for it was he who went to sleep and Coomara who walked off, as cool as a cucumber, he had better luck next time, for he looked out an extra strong drink he had, and he didn't play quite fair, he watered *his* down. At any rate old Coomara went sound asleep, so Jack nipped the cap off his head and ran down as fast as he could to Coomara's rock, and like a flash to the bottom of the sea. He carried out armfuls of the soul cages, turned each one upside down and shook it. He could see nothing except a tiny flickering light going up from each one, and a faint, faint sound like a far-away whistle. Then he carried all the cages back into the house and put them just as they had been. It was no easy matter for Jack to get off the bottom of the sea without Coomara to give him a back-up; but by a lucky chance a big cod put its tail down into the air below it, and Jack jumped up and caught its tail, and was carried through the sea in a flash. Old Coomara was still asleep when he got back, and when he waked he was so ashamed at having been beaten that he sneaked off without a word. But he never noticed that the soul cages were empty and he and Jack stayed great friends. Often when there was a storm Jack would make an excuse to slip down and rescue any new souls that were caught. One could say that Jack Dogherty had saved more souls than any priest in the whole countryside.

Muryans. *Muryan* is the Cornish word for "ant". The Cornish people used to think that the fairies were the souls of the heathen dead, who were not bad enough for Hell and not good enough for Heaven, so they had to stay on in this world. At first they were the size of ordinary men and women, but they had the power of changing into any bird they liked, and every time they changed back into their proper shape they were a little bit smaller, until they got as tiny as ants. After that they disappeared out of the state they were in, and no one knew quite what happend to them. This belief made the Cornishmen very careful about how they killed ants in case they destroyed a human soul. And indeed ants seem so wise that it is no wonder that people should think of them as fairies.

Nuckelavee. Nuckelavee was perhaps the horridest of all the monsters that were invented by the people of Britain. He was an Orkney sea-monster, a kind of horrible centaur. The lower part of him was a four-legged horse with fiery eyes and a terrible poisonous breath. Straight out of the back of this horse rose the body, arms and head of a man-like creature, the arms very long, so that they could almost sweep the ground, the head large, but rolling on its shoulders without a neck and very hideous; and the worst of it was that it had no skin, so that you could see its black veins running over its body, and its muscles and sinews knotting and contracting as it moved. It used to come out of the sea and ravage the countryside, devouring sheep and cattle and people, and destroying crops with its poisonous breath. There was one defence against it: it could not endure fresh water nor cross a running stream.

There was one old man called Tammas, who said that he had seen Nuckelavee in his youth, and after long persuasion he told someone about it. He was going home very late one moonlight night, and his shortest way was along a very narrow strip of land between the sea on one side and a deep lake on the other. The tide was full then, but even at a high tide the two waters never joined, so that it was safe to walk along between them; one was always fresh and the other always salt. He had got about halfway along when he saw in the moonlight a great, quick-moving thing coming towards him. He stopped and looked behind, wondering if he could get back to the open country before it could reach him. But it was coming too fast for that, and he had always been told that it was better to face an uncanny thing than to run from it. So he said a prayer to himself and went towards it. It came towards him, and he saw light streaming from two pairs of nostrils and from its horse's eyes. It was sweeping round with its great long arms to pick up anything it could find, but when it saw him it quickened its pace and came galloping forward. Tammas was a brave man, but it took all the courage he had to put one foot in front of another. They came abreast of each other and Nuckelavee swept out a long arm towards him, with long claws on each finger. Tammas leapt sideways to the edge of the lake, and the monster missed him. At the same time Tammas put one foot into the lake and the sweet, cool water splashed up all over him and wetted the monster, which shied away towards the sea as if it had been burnt. Tammas saw his chance and darted past it, close to the lake, and ran on as fast as he could.

He had remembered one chance of escape: there was a small outlet from the lake that emptied into the sea, not much more than a trickle but running fresh water, and if he could cross it he believed he would be safe. He ran like a madman. It seemed no more than three seconds before Nuckelavee swung round, howling with rage, and came thundering after him. Tammie saw the water ahead of him. Just as his feet touched the shingle the monster made a snatch at him. Tammie jumped the stream and fell fainting on the other side, whilst Nuckelavee stopped with a yell of rage and Tammie's cap in his hand.

Nursery Bogies. There are some terrifying creatures which seem to have been specially made up to warn children off dangerous ground or to keep them in order. It seems that most of them have never frightened grown-up people. They are sometimes called "frightening figures". Mrs Wright, who wrote a book called *Rustic Speech and Folk-Lore*, gives a whole list of them. Sometimes they are spoken of in threats: "If you dunna take care I'll show you Jack-up-the-Orchut," or, "Old Scratty'll get thee if thou doesn't come in!" or, "I'll send Mumpoker after ye!" – with a whole list more: Rawhead-and-Bloody-Bones, Tankerabogus, Tom Dockin, and

Tom-Poker. Then there are some that are meant to frighten children from stealing fruit or nuts: Lazy Laurence, A W D G O G G I E, the Gooseberry Wife, Churnmilk Peg, Melsh Dick; and others to prevent them tumbling into water: Grindylow, Jenny Greenteeth, and Nelly Longarms. No doubt these once played a useful part in keeping children out of danger, but no one over the age of ten would have been very likely to believe in them. They were a class in themselves.

Oisin. Oisin was the famous poet and singer of the great band of Irish warriors, the Fianna, and the last of them left alive. He was the son of Finn MacCool and of Sadbh, a fairy woman, who had been turned into a doe by the Dark Druid, Fear Doirche, who had been courting her in vain. She took refuge with the Fianna, where she could regain her woman's shape, and Finn loved her and married her. But when Finn was summoned to lead his band to war, the Dark Druid put on the appearance of Finn and lured her away, and though Finn searched everywhere he could never find her again. But one day when Finn was out hunting a great uproar arose among the pack, and when the hunters rode up they saw Finn's two favourite hounds protecting a beautiful little boy from

all the rest of the pack. Finn leapt from his horse and picked up the child. "O Oisin – my little fawn!" he said, for he knew Sadbh's child and his own son. Later when little Oisin could speak he told how he had been watched and nursed by a deer, and how a dark man had taken her away.

When he grew up Oisin became the sweetest singer and one of the most valiant fighters of the Fianna, and he lived to see the beginning of its dark days, for he fought in the Battle of Gabhra, where Osgar his son, who was next to him in valour, was killed. But one day the fairy princess, Niamh of the Golden Hair, fetched him away to Tir Nan Og, the Land of the Ever Young, and none of the Fianna ever saw him again. But hundreds of years after he had gone he came back, riding the white horse on which he had departed, but he returned to a changed world – the rivers were narrower and deeper, the hills were lower, the great Palace of Tara was a green mound, and there was not one of his companions among the weak and dwarfish men whom he saw tilling the countryside where the great forests had been. So with a sad heart he turned back towards the sea to return to Tir Nan Og and Niamh of the Golden Locks. As he went he passed a little group of the small, weak men whom he had already seen. They were struggling with all their might to lift a great stone trough, but their strength failed them to raise it by even an inch. His heart melted in him to see their helplessness. He had been told by Niamh that he must not set a foot to the ground, so he lent down in the saddle and was just lifting the trough easily enough when his saddle girth slipped and he fell down to the ground. The great white horse started and reared and thundered away to the sea, and where a golden youth had fallen from the saddle an old, old man lay on the ground, bent with the weight of many hundreds of years.

There was no return for Oisin to the Land of the Ever Young. And by that time Christianity had come to the land, and St Patrick was the great man there, and he listened eagerly to all that Oisin told him of the days of the Fianna. But though Patrick tried hard to win him to Christianity Oisin had no use for a Heaven in which there was no hunting or fighting, and he continued to lament the days of the Fianna until he died. But indeed we owe a great debt to Oisin, for if it had not been for him we should have none of the grand tales about Finn and the Fianna.

Old Man of Cury. There was once an old fisherman of Cury who was walking home one evening near Kynance Cove when he saw a girl sitting on a rock near a deep pool which had been deserted by the sea. He was thinking what a pretty girl she looked when suddenly she gave a start and slipped into the pool with a great splash. He ran round the rock as quick as he could and saw, to his surprise, that it was a MERMAID splashing about desperately in the pool. She burst into tears when she saw him looking down on her, and cried out, "Oh, Granfer, 'ee looks to have a kind face. Do, do, have pity on me and carry me over that terrible dry sand. I left my husband asleep and went to play in the surf, and I fell asleep in the hot sun and the sea has gone and left me stranded. Oh, do take me back. My husband is terrible savage and fierce when he's hungered, and I be in terrible fear he'll eat one of my pretty babes if I don't get back in time to give he his supper."

"Don't mention it my dear," said the old man. "Put your pretty arms round my neck and I'll heave you along in no time." She held tightly round his neck, and as he was walking along with her she asked him what three wishes she could give him as a reward for his kindness. "I've no need of money or grand ways," he said, "but I'd like the power to help others. Teach me the way to break spells and to know where stolen things be, and to cure illness, and I shall be right glad."

"That I will," she said, "for those be good wishes." She disentangled the comb from her hair and gave it to him. "Come back to this rock," she said, "when the moon's up tonight, and comb the water with my comb, and I'll be with you in a blink." With that she shot into the water, turned to kiss her hand and was gone. But that night when he combed the water she was there and told him all he wanted to know. And after that he often summoned her to advise him, and sometimes he carried her about on his back to see the land people walking about on their funny double tails. And he sometimes picked her land apples from the trees; but he never accepted her invitation to go and visit her under the water.

Pechs, or Picts. In the old days there used to be tales of a tribe of fairies in the Lowlands of Scotland who somehow came to be mixed up with the Picts, that race of whom so little is known and who are said to have built the Pictish earth houses and the Fingalian brochs, the high single towers with a window but no doors which

were entered by a rope ladder. The best remaining brochs are the church towers at Abernethy and Brechin. It used to be said about the Pechs: "They were wee, wee fowk, wi' red hair, and long, long arms, and feet sae braid that when it rained they could turn them up owre their heids, and they served for umbrellas. The

Pechs were great builders; they built a' the auld castles in the kintry." They were said to cut great blocks of stone in the quarry and then, standing in a long line, pass the stones from hand to hand over their heads, working so quickly that they would build a whole castle in a night. They were said to be three feet tall, which is a very common height for the fairies. There is a queer mixture of prehistoric men and fairies in these old traditions, and some people have a theory that the fairies of folklore were really the memories of early, conquered inhabitants remembered by the invaders. You will find a short account of them in Chambers's *Popular Rhymes of Scotland*.

Peg O'Nell. Peg O'Nell is the evil spirit of the river Ribble in Lancashire. One year in seven she is supposed to claim a life, and if a cat or dog has not been drowned to satisfy her she drowns a man or woman. There is a little spring in the grounds of Waddow Hall called Peg's Well after her, with a very old, headless statue by it, probably a Roman statue to the nymph of the Ribble, but the story that has grown up about Peg O'Nell is not so old as the statue. They say that there was once a rather cross, argumentative maid servant at Waddow Hall called Peg O'Nell. One cold, frosty night the mistress found that there was no water left in the kitchen, so she told Peg to take a bucket down to the well and fetch some. "I'm not going out on a wicked, perishing night like this," said Peg. "It's as black as pitch. Like enough I'll fall and break my neck." "You should have fetched the water before sunset," said her mistress. "Every pail and ewer in the house is dry." "You've no right to send me out like this," said Peg. "The path down to the well is a sheet of ice. If I go I'll break my neck as sure as Fate." And she went on grumbling until her mistress put the pail into her hand and said, "Out you go! Break your neck if you like, but I will have a pail of water." So out Peg went grumbling into the night, but she didn't come back; and when the farmhands went out with lanterns to look for her, there she was by the edge of the well with her neck broken. And every seven years Peg comes back to haunt Waddow Hall and claim a life for a life.

Peg Powler. No one has ever said that Peg Powler is a ghost; she
is a true-bred water-demon, the spirit of the River Tees, rather
like Jenny Greenteeth who haunted the rivers of Lancashire. She
has long green hair and she stretches long arms out of the water
to drag down children who venture too near the edge. The children
of Piercebridge used to be afraid that she would even leave the
water to carry them off. If Peg Powler was not invented by careful
mothers you may be sure that they made her sound as terrifying
as they could, for the Tees was a dangerous river.

People of Peace, or Daoine Sidhe. The People of Peace of the
Scottish Highlands are very much the same as the Daoine of
Ireland, except that we hear less of the fairy kings and queens in
Scotland than in Ireland. They are the trooping fairies of the
Highlands, who live under the green hills and ride on the Middle
Earth, hunting and dancing like other fairies. Some of them come
among mortals and seek human husbands and wives, generally
keeping their fairy blood a secret from other mortals. Many of the
Highland folk-collectors have stories of these People of Peace, and
the Lowland fairies are much like them, except that we hear more
of their kings and queens in the Lowlands, particularly of the

queens, Nicnevin or the Gyre-Carline. These fairy spirits often mixed with the witches in the sixteenth and seventeenth centuries, when witchcraft was much dreaded.

Phouka. The Phouka is the Irish PUCK. He is a great one for playing jokes on people, and many a ducking have men got for having made free with a pretty little pony and found themselves landed in a deep pool while the Phouka flourished off laughing, and many a fall have they got over a stick that suddenly thrust itself up from nowhere; but if men keep a friendly heart towards the Phouka, it may be he'll do them a good turn, and more than one. There is a good story told of the Phouka by Lady Wilde in her *Ancient*

Legends of Ireland, where you will find many good tales and some that are fearful too.

There was a boy called Phadrig, whose father was a farmer and a miller as well, and one day as he was minding his father's cattle something rushed past him like a whirlwind, but he was not in the least frightened, for he knew it was the Phouka going down to the mill, where the fairies used to meet after sunset; so he called out, "Phouka! Phouka! Show me what you are like, and I will give you my big coat to keep you warm!" Then the whirlwind spun round and came towards him in the form of a bull, lashing its tail like mad. But Phadrig stood his ground and threw his coat on it,

131

and it stopped at once, as meek as a lamb, and it said in a man's voice, "Come to the mill this night, Phadrig, when the moon is up, and you shall have good luck!"

So Phadrig went to the mill, and there were the sacks lying about on the floor waiting to be ground, and no one was grinding them, for the miller's men were all sound asleep. So Phadrig sat down and waited, but nothing happened, and a great drowsiness came on him and he fell asleep too, and when he waked it was daylight and the corn was all ground, but it was not the men who had done it, for they were still sound asleep. And this happened for three nights, and then Phadrig thought he would stay awake and watch.

There was an old chest in the mill, and that night Phadrig crept into it and pulled the lid gently down over his head, and watched through the big keyhole to see what would happen, and just at midnight six little men came in, each with a sack on his back, and they dumped them down by the other sacks, for the miller's men were all asleep as usual, and no one was grinding the corn. And after them came a little wizened old man in tattered rags of clothes, and he told them to start up the mill and grind the corn. And they started it and the old Phouka went among them and directed them, and before morning the corn was all ground.

In the morning the boy ran to his father and his father said he would watch with him, so that night they got into the big chest together, and all went as it had gone the night before. In the morning the miller said, "It's plain that all the work is done by the Phouka and the men are nothing but lazy louts; so I'll send the men away, and all the corn shall be ground by the good old Phouka."

So it was done, and the miller grew as rich as if he was grinding gold, for he had no wages to pay and all he ground was clear profit; but he never told how his money came, for fairy gifts must not be told. Now Phadrig had a great liking for the old Phouka, and he used often to get into the chest to watch him, and it went to his heart to see him so tattered and worn and having such a work with the idle young phoukas, who scamped the work all they could, and he had to be forever after them. And Phadrig thought to himself at least he'd get him good clothes to keep him warm in the chilly mill-house. There was plenty of money going, so Phadrig bought a fine suit of good cloth and a silk waistcoat for the old Phouka and laid it ready on the floor just where old Phouka used to stand. At midnight the Phouka came in and saw the suit. "What's that?" he said. "It's surely left for me!" He put it on and strutted up and down the place as pleased as Punch. Suddenly he remembered the corn to be ground and turned towards the mill. "No, no!" he said. "I'm a fine gentleman now, and gentlemen don't grind corn. No, no, I'll out into the world and make a grand show there." And he kicked his old rags into a corner and strolled out with a grand air.

No more work was done in the mill that night, nor on any night after. When the old Phouka had gone, the little phoukas ran away, but the miller had grown so rich that he could afford to sell his mill and farm, build a fine house and send his son to college; so Phadrig grew into a good scholar and a handsome gentleman, but he greatly missed his old friend. Many a night he would wander in the fields calling, "Phouka, Phouka. Let me get a sight of you! I'm missing you sorely!" It was no use, he never set eyes on the Phouka again. Yet for all that the Phouka had not forgotten him. When Phadrig had left college and was a grand young gentleman with a house of his own, he married a young lady, so sweet and beautiful that people said she was like a daughter of the Fairy King, and among the drinks on the table there stood a golden goblet full of most fragrant wine. No one knew where it came from, but Phadrig was sure that it was a wedding present from his old friend, the Phouka. He was not afraid to drink it. He lifted it up and pledged his bride, and made her pledge him in return, and all their lives they had good fortune and health and happiness, for the love of the Phouka was on them. As for the golden goblet, Phadrig kept it, and his son after him, and it has been kept as a treasure in his family till this day.

Pixies, or Piskies. Pixies, Pigsies and Piskies are the merry, mischievous fairies of Somerset, Devon and Cornwall. They are rather different to look at in different counties, but they are much the same in character. The Somerset pixies sometimes appear the size of ordinary humans, though they are generally about the size of a man's hand. Whatever size they are, they all have red hair and turned-up noses, squinting eyes and wide mouths. They wear green clothes. The Devon pigsies are little and pale and slim and they wear no clothes at all. The Cornish piskies are like little old men, very withered and wearing green rags, like the old PHOUKA in Lady Wilde's story. In the Midlands, PUCKS and pouks are very like pixies, very fond of playing practical jokes, and Will o' the

Wisp tricks in particular, but though they are mischievous they are on the whole kind, and often do work about the house and the farm like BROWNIES. In fact, they may be counted among the good fairies, the SEELIE COURT.

Puck. Puck is Shakespeare's picture of the Midland puck who plays bogie-beast pranks, changing his shape like the HEDLEY KOW or the Picktree BRAG, and misleading night travellers like Jack o' Lantern. Puck says that he sometimes takes the shape of a roasted crab-apple in a punch-bowl in the hands of an old wife, and bobs about till he spills the drink over her chin, or makes himself look

like a three-legged stool and then slips away from under the old gossip who is sitting down on it. Or he takes the shape of a young filly and leads away a staid old horse with his rider on his back, or "misleads night wanderers, laughing at their harm". But for all that he is really rather fond of human beings and is sorry for the two young girls who are lost and frightened in the forest, unkindly treated by their true-loves. Like most fairies he is always ready for a joke, but he is not one to carry it too far. Very often in masques and pictures Puck would be given goats' legs and feet and little horns on his head, like the classical satyrs.

Redcaps. Redcaps are some of the wickedest of the evil fairies. They live on the Borders between England and Scotland, where there always used to be much fighting and many wicked deeds were done, and they liked to live in old peel towers or half-ruined castles where there has been much slaughter. Often only one redcap lives in the place at a time, and he is described as an old, broad-shouldered man, very strong, with long, sticking-out teeth and skinny arms and hands, armed with long talons like an eagle's claws. He wears iron boots and carries a pike-staff in his left hand. On his head there is a rusty red cap and it is his delight to dye the cap a brighter red in the blood of any benighted traveller who tries to shelter in the tower. No human strength can prevail against him but he can be frightened away by quoting from the Bible or by showing him a cross. If a cross is held up to him he gives a dismal yell and disappears, leaving one of his long teeth behind him. There is one good redcap known who lives in Grantully Castle in Perthshire. He has a little room of his own at the top of the castle, and it is lucky to have him in the place; but he is not at all like the Border redcaps. (See illustration opposite)

Roane. *Roane* is the Gaelic name for seals, but the Highland people used to believe that these seals were not animals but fairy people, and that they wore the skins to pass through the water. In this they were like the SELKIES of Orkney and Shetland and the MERROWS of Ireland, except that the merrows used red caps instead of covering skins. The Roane were the kindest of all fairy people, for

they do not seem to have avenged themselves even on the mortals
who spent their lives in hunting and killing them.

There is a story of a man who lived near John o' Groats that
shows this very clearly. This man was a skilful fisherman and was
the most expert seal-fisher in all the country round. But the most
successful sportsman has his times of bad luck, and one evening
the seal-fisher was returning home in low spirits, for he had lost
a great dog-seal which he had struck, and the creature had made
its escape with the fisher's favourite gully-knife stuck in its haunch.
By his cottage door in the dusk a stranger was waiting for him,
mounted on a magnificent horse. "Good evening friend," said the
stranger. "Are you Peter Ruach, the seal-fisher?" "I am, sir," said
the fisher. "Then come with me," said the stranger. "A friend has
sent me to you to make a bargain for a large number of sealskins.

Get up behind me and I will take you to the place where he is waiting." He pulled Peter up, and they set off as fast as the wind, faster indeed, for the wind, which blew behind them, seemed to be in their faces. They rode straight towards the sea, and at the edge of a great cliff the stranger reined in his horse. "We dismount here," he said. "My friend is waiting for us." "But where is he?" said the seal-fisher. "There is no house near here." "He is just below," said the stranger, and he seized Peter Ruach in a mighty grip and leapt with him over the cliff. Down, down they went through the air, with the wind whistling in their ears, then splash into the sea and down, down, with the water swirling round them, until they reached a door in the cliff-face. The stranger pushed it open and Peter found himself in a place of long passages and caves, inhabited by sad, gentle seal-people, and when he looked at the man beside him, he saw that he was a man no longer, but a seal, and when he glanced down at himself he saw that he was in the form of a seal too.

Then Peter was filled with terror when he thought how he had killed dozens, no, scores, of their people – their brothers, fathers, mothers, perhaps – and by what a cruel punishment they might justly avenge themselves. The roane saw his terror and seemed to pity him, for they gently murmured, "Do not be afraid, we mean you no harm." But the seal-fisher saw his guide draw out a great clasp knife and was sure that it was to be used on him. His last drop of courage ebbed out of him, and he flung himself down and begged to be spared. "Do not be afraid," said their guide. "I mean you no harm. Tell me, is this knife yours?" The fisher saw that it was his own gully-knife that he had lost that day. He looked in the great soft eyes of his captor and said, "Yes, it was mine." A murmur of joy went round the company, and his captor said, "Then you have it in your power to save my father's life. He escaped today with this knife still lodged in him and he is now dying in great pain. Only you can save him. Come with me." He led the seal-fisher to an inner cave, and there on a sort of couch a big dog-seal lay in great pain. They bared his wound. "Do you wish with all your heart that he was healed?" said the son. "That I do," said Peter Ruach. "I did not know what I was doing." "Then take this knife and make a light scratch round the wound, wishing with all your heart that it was healed." Peter took the knife and did as he was told, and as he drew the circle the wound closed up, the pain and fever died away, and the old seal rose up from his bed as well as he had ever been.

There was such joy in that sad company as had never been before, but among them the seal-fisher was sad, for he thought that even if they were too gentle to kill him he could never get back to the light of the sun and to his wife and children. But the roane saw his trouble and said, "My horse is waiting on the cliff-top. I can take you up, but there is one condition: you must vow the most solemn vow you know that you will never kill or injure one of the Roane. The fish of the sea you may catch for your living, but from now on the Roane are sacred to you." "May my hands drop off and fall into the sea," said Peter Ruach, "if I ever touch one of the Roane people to do them the least injury, for they have been noble friends to me this night." He touched hands solemnly with the father and the son, and was borne up even more swiftly than he had gone down to the top of the cliff. There the roane became a man again, breathed on him, and gave him back his human shape. The two rode as quick as light to the cottage door and parted. But before he turned away the seal-man gave Peter a bag of gold pieces which well repaid him for the loss of any seal-skins he could win in a long life.

It is an old belief that a deadly wound can only be cured by means of the weapon that made it, in the hand that struck the blow.

Robin Goodfellow. In the sixteenth century Robin Goodfellow was the most famous of the hobgoblins. Shakespeare even makes "Robin Goodfellow" Puck's nickname, and there are many short rhymes about him and mentions of him in poems and pamphlets. There is a chapbook – that is something like our cheaper paper-backs – called *Robin Goodfellow – His Mad Pranks and Merry Jests*, which was first printed in 1628 and gives a short life of Robin Goodfellow. According to this he was a half-fairy: his father was Oberon the King of the Fairies and his mother was a pretty

country girl. All kinds of rich presents and nice food were left for him by the fairies when he was a baby, and he was the most mischievous little imp you can imagine, though he had no magical powers; but by the time he was six years old his mother could hardly bear him in the house, so he determined to run away and seek his fortune. He fell asleep by the roadside and the fairies came and talked to him in his sleep. When he woke up be found that it was no dream, for a golden scroll was lying beside him telling him that he was Oberon's son, and Oberon was giving him the power to change his shape into anything he liked and to have whatever he wished for. He told him that those powers should be used to punish wicked people and to reward good ones, and that if he used them worthily his father would come and take him into Fairyland.

So provided for he started on his career as a hobgoblin, and each chapter tells about one of his pranks, each ending with his going away singing, and laughing "Ho! Ho! Ho!" At one time people used to say, "laughing like a Robin Goodfellow". At length he is taken into Fairyland, where he joins a fairy-ring with little Tom Thumb as the piper, and the fairies give short accounts of what they do and what they are called, each finishing with a little song. There are many half-mortals in the fairy traditions but Robin Goodfellow is one of the most famous.

Seelie Court. In Scotland the good fairies were called the "Seelie Court". *Seelie* is the old Saxon word for "blessed". The wicked fairies were called the UNSEELIE COURT and they were bad indeed. It was not safe to offend even good fairies, for they could punish offences pretty sharply, but on the whole they had kindly feelings towards human beings. They helped the poor and made the corn grow and always repaid kindnesses. They found lost children and led them home, and if people were kind and cheerful and polite the fairies helped them on their way and brought them good fortune. These were often kindnesses from a single fairy to a single human, but by the "Seelie Court" people generally meant the good trooping fairies who rode through the country blessing the fields, and visited human houses that were left ready for them with the hearth swept and the fire bright and clean water so that the fairy babies could be washed, and where they could dance and sing with no curious eyes watching them. They left a blessing behind them in such places, always good fortune and prosperity, and sometimes a silver sixpence in the shoe of the maid who had left everything neat and ready.

When the Fairy Queen rode by with her court she sometimes righted wrongs and undid enchantments. A story of that kind is told in the old ballad of Alison Gross.

Alison Gross was an evil and ugly witch who fell in love with a handsome young knight and promised him all kinds of wealth if he would be her lover. He was too good to love such a wicked creature and too truthful to put her off with false promises. "Away,

away, you ugly witch!" he cried at last. "I wouldn't kiss your ugly mouth for all the gold you could offer me!" At that she turned round three times and struck the knight with a silver wand, and he changed into a loathsome-looking worm and wound himself about a tree. No one cared for him but his sister, who came to him every Saturday night and washed his ugly face in a silver basin and combed his strange snaky locks with a silver comb. But for all she did she could not disenchant him, until one Halloween the Seelie Court came riding by with the Fairy Queen at its head, and at the sight of the poor worm winding itself round the tree the Queen dismounted from her horse, sat down on a bank of daisies and beckoned the poor knight to her side. He came sliding over to her and she lifted the ugly head on her knee and stroked him three times, and at once his serpent shape shrivelled away and a handsome knight was kneeling in front of her. And after the Queen's touch Alison Gross had no more power over him. That was the work of the Seelie Court at its best.

Selkies. The selkies are the seal people of Orkney and Shetland, very like the ROANE of the Highlands. In these Islands the ordinary common seal, which they call the "tang fish", is not supposed to be a fairy creature, but the sea-lions, the crested seals, the grey seals and all the larger ones are thought to be fairy people who live on a dry land under the sea or on lonely skerries, and wear sealskins to move through the water like the MERROWS and ROANE. They are generally thought to be Fallen Angels, who were driven out of Heaven for their allegiance to Satan but were not bad enough for Hell. In their human form they are very beautiful and the male selkies used to come courting mortal women. The female selkies were content with their own husbands, but they used to come on to the smooth sands to dance, and then they would take off the skins and lay them aside, and quite often it happened that a mortal would see them and fall in love with one. Then he had only to steal away her skin and she was a captive and was forced in the end to marry him. These selkie women made good wives and tender mothers, but their hearts were always with their real husbands and in the end the skin would be found and they

would hurry away to their underwater country. If they saw their husbands on the way they would speak kindly to them, but their hearts were always with their first loves, and it was right that it should be so.

Shock. A shock is a Suffolk bogie-beast, which can take the form of a horse or a donkey, or sometimes a great dog or a calf. It can do physical harm as well as causing great terror. There is an old story told of how a countryman, Goodman Kemp of Woodbridge, burst into the Horse and Groom at Melton on one dark winter's night and asked for the loan of a gun to shoot a shock which was swinging on the toll-gate bars. He said it had the head of a donkey and a smooth velvet hide. All the guests came out with him to see the beast, and this made him so bold that he tried to seize it and drag it into the light, so that they could see what it was like. But it turned and gave him such a bite that he bore the mark of it all

Silky

his life. In other stories the shock takes the form of a ghostly funeral.

Silky. BROWNIES are nearly all male spirits, though there is one famous female brownie called Meg Mullach, "Hairy Meg", who attached herself long ago to the Grants of Tullochgorn, and stories have been told about her quite recently. But the silkies of Northumberland behave just like brownies, and they are always female. A silky was a spirit dressed in rustling white silk, who did all kinds of jobs about the house and was a terror to idle servants. She was generally thought of as a kind of ghost, like the CAULD LAD OF HILTON.

One of the most famous of the Silkies lived at Heddon Hall in the nineteenth century, but she seemed more mischievous than helpful, for though she tidied what was left untidy, she would often throw about anything that had been neatly arranged. When her domestic work was done she used to spend a great part of the night sitting in an old tree near the drive, and from there she used to amuse herself by stopping carts and carriages and halting horses. She could do nothing, however, against anyone who held

up a rowan-wood cross. Even after her hauntings had ceased, the tree used to be called "Silky's Chair". Her hauntings came to an end one day when a ceiling in Heddon Hall gave way and a large, rough skin filled with gold fell into the room below. After that the silky was never seen or heard again. So people thought that she must have been the ghost of someone who had hidden the treasure and had died without telling anyone about it.

There was another silky who lived at Denton Hall near Newcastle. She is mentioned in one of the nineteenth-century folklore books, but there is later news of her than that, for a friend from the North Country told me that when she was a girl she used to go with her mother to visit two old ladies, the Hoyles of Denton, who sometimes talked to their close friends about the silky. It was a big, rambling house and they said they did not know what they would do without Silky. She used to sweep and clean, and lay and light fires, and there was something too about little bunches of flowers left on the stairs.

My friend grew up and married and went to live in the South, and it was not till the Second World War that she visited Denton Hall again. The two old ladies had died long ago and the Hall had been leased to another old friend of hers – they had gone to the same dancing class together when they were children. She said that he was not at all the kind of person to get on with a household spirit. Silky could not stand him and she was playing the most terrible practical jokes on him, and in the end he had to leave the house. Poor Silky had stopped being a Brownie and become a BOGGART.

Skillywidden. Once there was a Cornish farmer cutting furze for thatching, and among the furze-brakes he came on a patch of heather – "griglans", he called it – and stretched on it sound asleep there was a little fairy, not more than a foot in length. The farmer picked the little fellow up, very carefully so as not to wake him, took off his hedging cuff, slipped him into it, and carried him home, where he shut the door carefully and emptied him out on to the hearthstone. He woke up, all alert in a moment, and began to play with the children, who were delighted with their little "Bobby

Griglans", as they called him. The farmer and his wife determined to keep Bobby Griglans to themselves, for they hoped he would show them where the fairies' treasure hoards were on the hillside, so they took care to keep him in the house and to let none of the neighbours see him. But in a day or two the farmer had finished his furze-cutting, and it was time for the neighbours to come in and help to carry the bundles of furze down from the hillside and build them into stacks according to custom. The farmer and his wife were afraid the children would talk, so they put them and Bobby Griglans into the big barn.

While the furze-carriers were at their dinner and the yard was quiet, little Bobby Griglans piped up, "Lift I up and I can fiddle the lock for 'ee and us can have a courant round the furze-reeks."

No sooner said than done, and they were out in the yard in no time. There was a half-finished stack in front of them and the first thing they saw was a little man and woman, not twice the size of little Bobby, searching and peering about among the scattered bundles of furze. The little woman was wringing her hands and crying out, "Oh, my dear and tender Skillywidden, wherever canst ah be gone to? Shall I never cast eyes on thee again?" "Go 'ee back," said Bob to the children. "There's my Father and Mother."

And he piped out, "Here I am, Mammy." Before the words were out of his mouth, the three had popped into a hole out of sight. The children got a whipping, but it was worth it to think of little Skillywidden back with his father and mother again.

Spriggans. Spriggans were Cornish BOGIES. They were very hideous and fierce, and were the fairies' bodyguard. If anyone insulted or tried to rob the fairies, the spriggans would suddenly appear and march out to their defence. Cornishmen said that they were the ghosts of the old GIANTS killed by the Britons who first invaded this country, and this seems strange because the spriggans were generally small, but they could swell themselves to a great size when they went to fight.

In the story of the "FAIRIES ON THE EASTERN GREEN" it was the spriggans who marched out to avenge the insult shouted by the smuggler at the old fairy pipers, and at every step forward they grew larger and more terrible.

Trows. The trows of Shetland are something like the smaller Scandinavian trolls – not, of course, the many-headed giants, but the trolls who are rather smaller than mortal men, malicious, mischievous creatures who, like the giant trolls, are turned to stone by the light of the sun. The Shetland trows dread the sun too, but it harms them less than the trolls. If, by any mistake, they stay on the upper earth after sunrise they cannot escape all day, but wander about, frightened and trying to hide, muttering to themselves, as much afraid of man as men are of them.

Jessie Saxby told us most of what we know about the Shetland trows in her book *Shetland Traditional Lore*. She was a Shetlander herself, and was the ninth child of a ninth child, which is a very special thing. The Shetlanders think it very unlucky to talk of the trows, but the old people would tell things to Jessie Saxby which they would not tell to any other child.

It is she who tells us about the "kunal trows", that is, the king trows, who are a peculiar breed. There are no females among them and they are forced to take mortal women as wives, but as soon as the baby trow is born the mother dies. Kunal trows never marry again, so every kunal trow is forced to live a solitary life until his son is full grown, and then he too dies. Sometimes they try the experiment of refusing to marry so that they can live for ever, but that is against the laws of Trowland, and those who do not marry when they get to the proper age are driven into exile. One old kunal trow defied the law and lived for centuries in a ruined broch, the terror of the countryside, but at length a young witch, who wanted to learn magic secrets from him, persuaded him to marry her. She did not enjoy her wedded life, however, for whenever she visited her mother she told her how mortal maidens could be protected against the "grey woman-stealers". By her magical arts the witch seems to have protected herself against dying when her child was born, for she and her husband had several children.

The other trows were more like ordinary fairies, and like all fairies they were great lovers of music. They were little people, clothed in grey. The men always walked backwards when they saw humans, to keep them under observation. It was thought lucky to hear trows talking, but very unlucky to see them. People were afraid of them, but when they took a fancy to someone they were very ready to do him good. There was one in particular called "Broonie", who looked after all the farms in one small area, and people used to see him at night flitting from field to field and bringing good luck and fertility wherever he went. The women grew sorry for him going continually through the bitter wind in his thin grey rags, and they consulted together and made him a cloak and hood. But he resented this like any other BROWNIE and left the farmlands for ever.

It seems that people were more frightened than need be by their odd looks and uncouth ways, for the little trows seem to be in their hearts rather friendly to humans.

Tylweth Teg. The ordinary fairy people of Wales are generally called the "Tylweth Teg", that is, the "Fair Family", though occasionally they are called BENDITH Y MAMAU (the "Mother's Blessing"), in an attempt to persuade them not to kidnap human babies, which they are very apt to do. They are fair-haired and very much admire golden-haired children, whom they carry away into Fairyland if they can. They live under green hills or under water and love dancing, singing and music like other fairies. The fairy maidens are easily won as wives and will live with human husbands for a time. The danger of visiting the Tylweth Teg in their own country is that time passes at a miraculous rate in Fairyland, and their guest is apt to find that a hundred years of mortal time has passed in what he believed to be less than a hundred minutes. The Tylweth Teg give rich gifts sometimes to their favourites, but these vanish if they are spoken of. Indeed, the Tylweth Teg are very much like the fairies everywhere.

Unseelie Court. The "Unseelie Court" is the name given in Scotland
to the wicked fairies who do all they can to hurt, frighten and
destroy human mortals. Even the SEELIE COURT, the good fairies,
can be quite dangerous if they are annoyed, but the Unseelie Court
are never kind to human beings, even if they are kindly treated.
In the Fen Country there is a story of a little fairy called Yallery

Brown whom a kind labourer had rescued out of a bottle where he had been imprisoned, but who, though he pretended he was going to reward the man, went out of his way to damage him and spoil his luck in every possible way. Little Yallery Brown was a perfect picture of one of the Unseelie Court. But the "Host" of the Highlands are the most typical of all, for they go about in great crowds as thick as starlings and snatch up unfortunate men and women who have got into their power, forcing them to shoot fairy darts at people and cattle whom they overtake on the flight, and spreading blight over crops and pestilence over sheep and cattle. There are other solitary evil creatures, the NUCKELAVEE, DUERGARS, REDCAPS and the like, against which people used to carry about crusts of bread, crosses made of ash or rowan, an open knife, and other protections against evil spirits. One cannot stay too far from the Unseelie Court, but courage, an innocent heart and a devout prayer can protect a traveller from all these threats of evil.

Urisks. The urisk was a kind of rough BROWNIE who lived in the Highlands of Scotland. He was rather like a satyr to look at – like

a hairy man above, and with the hind legs and hoofs of a goat. He was very lucky to have about the house, where he did all kinds of household jobs as well as working about the farm and herding the sheep and cattle. He often had a favourite pool that he haunted, but he was sometimes lonely for human company and would follow a traveller all night. The traveller was generally terrified, for he did not know how harmless and affectionate the urisk was. Urisks lived as solitary fairies, but several times a year they would have meetings. Their favourite meeting place was a corrie near Loch Katrine.

Wild Edric. There are many stories of mortal men who married fairy wives, but the earliest of all is about Wild Edric, the champion who lived in Shropshire and stood out against William the Norman when he invaded England. One day Edric was hunting in the Forest of Clun when he became separated from the rest of the hunt and wandered for hours in the deep forest with only a little page for company. It had grown dark when they saw a light in the distance and made their way to a large and fair house from which light streamed out and music sounded. They looked in through

the windows and saw a great company of most beautiful ladies dancing. They were taller and more beautiful than mortal women, and there was one of them more beautiful than all the rest. When he saw her Edric was enflamed with love, and he wanted nothing in the world except to have her for his wife. He ran round the castle until he found a way in, burst into the dance room, followed by his brave little page, seized the lady and began to carry her away. All her sisters attacked him with tooth and nail, but he cared nothing for them and at length, bleeding and torn, he and the page made their way out and carried off the lady between them, back to Edric's castle.

For three days the lady lay silent in the room where Wild Edric had put her, while he wooed her with everything he had or could offer her. On the fourth day she suddenly spoke. "You have conquered, my dear," she said. "I will be your wife, and we shall be happy and fortunate together as long as you never reproach me with my sisters, or the place from which you brought me. On the day that you do that I warn you solemnly that I shall vanish from you for ever, and all our happiness and prosperity will vanish with me."

Edric vowed solemnly that he would be her true and loving husband and would never reproach her, and they were married with great solemnity before a company of all the nobles of the countryside. By this time Wild Edric had submitted to William the Norman, since Harold was dead and there was no one to take his place, and the Norman heard of the strange wedding and summoned Edric and his wife, the Lady Godda, to his Court. They came, and everyone marvelled at her beauty, and after that they had many happy years together, and fair and loving children.

There was only one thing that fretted Edric, and that was that every now and then, when her husband wanted her most, she would be absent and not to be found. One day he returned from hunting, longing to spread out his game in front of her and tell her the adventures of the day. She was nowhere to be found. He hunted high and low, in every nook and corner; she was nowhere. At length, looking from the battlements, he saw her hurrying towards the castle. He thundered down the stairs and met her on the drawbridge. "Where have you been?" he said. "You must have been with your sisters." He would have said more, but he spoke to empty air. She had vanished. He searched all over the Forest of Clun, looking in vain for the great house that had stood there.

He never saw her again on this side of the grave. Worn out and broken-hearted he died, still searching. But tradition has it that he rejoined his lady on the other side of the grave, for Wild Edric and his lady have been seen from time to time riding together at the head of their company. Quite late in the nineteenth century a maid told her mistress that as a girl she had seen Wild Edric and his followers riding by, and she described their clothes, and it was the Saxon dress they were wearing. The miners round the Forest of Clun believed that war and troubles were coming on the country when Wild Edric rode. And it was fitting that he should come to warn them, for in his day he had been the great champion of the Welsh Border.

BIBLIOGRAPHY

BRIGGS, K. M., *The Personnel of Fairyland*, The Alden Press, Oxford, 1969; Gale Research Co., Detroit, 1971. (Brownies, boggarts, mermaids.)

BRIGGS, K. M., and TONGUE, RUTH L. (eds.), *The Folktales of England*, Routledge & Kegan Paul, London, 1963; University of Chicago Press, 1965. (Apple-Tree Man.)

BROOME, DORA, *Fairy Tales from the Isle of Man*, Penguin Books, Harmondsworth, 1951; Norris Modern Press, Douglas, Isle of Man. (Dooinney-oie.)

CHAMBERS, ROBERT, *Popular Rhymes of Scotland*, W. & R. Chambers, Edinburgh, 1870; Gale Research Co., Detroit, 1969. (Elves, pechs.)

COURTNEY, MARGARET, *Cornish Feasts and Folklore*, Beare & Son, Penzance, 1890; Rowman & Littlefield, Totowa, New Jersey. (Bucca.)

CROKER, T. CROFTON, *Fairy legends and Traditions of the South of Ireland*, 3 vols., John Murray, London, 1825–8; facsimile edition, Lemma Publishing Corporation, New York, 1976: U.K. distributor Colin Smythe Ltd, Gerrards Cross, Bucks. (Lepracaun, cluricaune.)

DOUGLAS, GEORGE, *Scottish Fairy and Folk Tales*, Walter Scott, London, 1893; Arno Press, New York, 1977. (Nuckelavee, Laird of Lorntie, Roane.)

GRICE, F., *Folk Tales of the North Country*, Nelson, London and Edinburgh, 1944. (Duergars.)

HARTLAND, E. S., *English Fairy and Folk Tales*, Walter Scott, London, 1893; Gale Research Co., Detroit, 1968. (Skillywidden, Colman Grey, Green Children.)

Bibliography

HENDERSON, WILLIAM, *Folk-Lore of the Northern Counties*, Folk-Lore Society, London, 1879; E. P. Publishing, East Ardsley, Wakefield, W. Yorks., 1973; Rowman & Littlefield, Totowa, New Jersey, 1973. (Barguest, dunters.)

HUNT, ROBERT, *Popular Romances of the West of England*, Hotten, London, 1865; Chatto & Windus, London, 1923; Arno Press, New York, 1968. (Pixies, giants.)

JACOBS, JOSEPH, *English Fairy Tales*, Nutt, London, 1890; Schocken Books, New York, 1967; Puffin Books, Harmondsworth, 1970. *More English Fairy Tales*, Nutt, London, 1894; Schocken Books, New York, 1969: U.K. distributor Wildwood House, London. (Yallery Brown, Tom Tit Tot.)

MACDONALD, GEORGE, *The Princess and the Goblin*, Blackie, Glasgow, undated; Puffin Books, Harmondsworth and New York, 1964, 1970. (Goblins.)

RHYS, JOHN, *Celtic Folk-Lore, Welsh and Manx*, 2 vols., Oxford University Press, 1901; 1-vol. edition, Arno Press, New York, 1972. (Bendith y Mamau, bwca, fairy brides.)

SAXBY, JESSIE M.E., *Shetland Traditional Lore*, reprint, Norwood Editions, Norwood, Pennsylvania, 1974. (Trows.)

SIKES, WIRT, *British Goblins*, Sampson Low, London, 1880; facsimile edition, E.P. Publishing, East Ardsley, Wakefield, W. Yorks., 1973; Charles River Books, Boston, Massachusetts, 1976. (Coblynau.)

TOLKIEN, J.R.R., *The Hobbit,* Allen & Unwin, London, 1937; paperback, 1966; Houghton Mifflin, Boston, Massachusetts, 1938; Ballantine Books (paperback), New York, 1976. (Dragon, goblins.)

TONGUE, RUTH L., *Forgotten Folk-Tales of the English Counties*, Routledge & Kegan Paul, London and New York, 1970. (Black Annis.)

WILDE, LADY, *Ancient Legends, Mystic Charms and Superstitions of Ireland,* 2 vols., Ward & Downey, London, 1887; O'Gorman, Galway, 1975: U.K. distributor Colin Smythe Ltd, Gerrards Cross, Bucks. (Changelings, Daoine Sidhe, Phouka.)

WRIGHT, E. M., *Rustic Speech and Folk-Lore,* Oxford University Press, 1913; Gale Research Co., Detroit, 1968. (Nursery bogies.)

YEATS, W. B., *Irish Fairy and Folk-Tales,* Walter Scott, London, 1893; Colin Smythe Ltd, Gerrards Cross, Bucks., 1973; AMS Press, New York, 1977. (Daoine Sidhe.)

About the Author and the Artist

Katharine Briggs, internationally hailed as one of Britain's most eminent folklore scholars, was born in 1898, one of the three daughters of water-colorist Ernest Briggs. She studied English at Oxford, earning her Ph.D. with a thesis on folklore in seventeenth-century literature, and became a D.Litt., Oxon., in 1969. Her many books on folklore include *An Encyclopedia of Fairies, British Folktales,* and *The Vanishing People,* all published by Pantheon. She is currently working on a book on cat lore, which Pantheon will publish in 1980, and a book on the folklore of women through the centuries.

Dr. Briggs is a past president and honorary life-member of the English Folklore Society. She has also taught and lectured at several American universities and is an honorary member of the American Folklore Society.

Yvonne Gilbert was born in Northumberland in 1951. Her work has appeared in several British magazines and on numerous book jackets; *Abbey Lubbers, Banshees, and Boggarts* is her first full-length endeavor and marks her first appearance in the United States. Ms. Gilbert lives in Liverpool, England.